How to

Let your

Genie

Out

and manifest your
heart's desires

Shirley Crichton

ecademyPRESS
www.ecademy-press.com

How To Let Your Genie Out
and manifest your heart's desires

First published in 2012 by

Ecademy Press
48 St Vincent Drive, St Albans, Herts, AL1 5SJ
info@ecademy-press.com
www.ecademy-press.com

Available online and from all good bookstores

Cover design by Shirley Crichton
Artwork by Karen Gladwell
Author photo by Dom Jones, www.dombjones.com

Printed on acid-free paper from managed forests.
This book is printed on demand, so no copies will
be remaindered or pulped.

ISBN 978-1-908746-50-4

To Terence,

Becca and Daniel,

Oli and Xander,

who light my life.

Acknowledgements

With gratitude to all who have helped me in producing this book.

To my family, friends and colleagues for your wonderful encouragement and support during this process.

To the generous group who read my first draft and so enthusiastically gave me valuable feedback on my embryo book.

To Emma and all the Ecademy Press magicians for their help and expertise in bringing this book to you.

To the Book Midwife, Mindy Gibbins-Klein, for her inspiration, knowledge and wisdom as she helped me to negotiate this unknown territory of writing a book.

To all of my clients over the years who have helped me to learn what I share today.

To the Genie in us all.

Contents

My Route To Happiness

Everybody wants to be happy. This is a simple conclusion I have come to after twenty-five years of studying and practising many different forms of self-help, personal development, spiritual beliefs and traditions, healing methods and new age philosophies. I have investigated all manner of traditional through to really way-out systems of understanding and exploring what helps people to live a life which is meaningful and enjoyable to them.

This all began as I approached forty. On the face of it, my life at that time was pretty good. I had recently set up and was running a boarding kennels which was becoming very successful. I had been married to Terence for nearly twenty years, having the usual ups and downs of most marriages, but on the whole we were trundling along together. I was also mother to two teenagers, with all the joys and challenges that brings.

As things settled down after the excitement of starting a new business and seeing it take off, I suddenly began considering how my life really was at a deeper level. This was a new experience for me, but not uncommon, I understand, as I approached what was considered 'the big four-o'. Well, it was considered a big milestone in those days.

I began to realise that although I had very strong opinions about most things, considering that I was right and anyone who held differing opinions was wrong, underneath it all I actually wasn't very happy.

This came as a big shock. I was living the life I chose, working hard and I had a lovely Mercedes car to drive around in. So how come I wasn't happy?

A friend of mine had been taking a counselling course for a couple of years or so. She used to tell me about it and I was very dismissive, thinking it all a load of nonsense. Eventually it occurred to me that maybe, just maybe, I wasn't as 'right' as I thought I was and that perhaps, just perhaps, if I modified some of my attitudes and thinking, I might be happier. This was radical after many years of putting so much time and effort into being right.

So I, too, took the counselling course and was introduced to some very challenging ideas, but, resist as I might, I began to see how I had been limiting myself and what a narrow view of life and the world I had been holding. I became fascinated by the possibilities that were opening up for me as I gained some understanding of how I had been operating in life. I was hooked and wanted to learn more.

This counselling training led to studying and a career in stress management and hypnotherapy, which I found very rewarding. This was followed by NLP, which is a very practical, fun and amazingly effective approach to creating change. To my surprise, this subsequently led on to Reiki healing, working with Angels, running workshops and training as an Interfaith Minister – an amazing development for someone who had been a hostile atheist, with very strong, unfavourable views about people who believed in anything that could not be explained and understood in our three-dimensional 'real' world.

Terence and I have had many adventures, travelling to amazing places and learning from some very gifted teachers along the way.

Over the years, I have met and had the privilege of working with thousands of people who were in some way unhappy with their lives and wanting to make changes. This book is a distillation of essential aspects of facilitating change and creating the life you want which have worked well for me and my clients. I have tremendous respect and appreciation for all the clients, members of the audience when I have given talks and participants in trainings and workshops I have run. I am constantly inspired by the resilience of the human spirit and the ability to move on, whatever life throws up, and to create happiness and success.

I speak from my own experience as my life has progressed in ways I would not have believed possible when this intentional journey began. In a way, this is the book I would have liked to have had available along the way. However, if it had been available to me then, I might not have had the wonderful adventures I have enjoyed so much. All my experiences have been part of a journey which has brought me to a place where I am very happy. So happy, in fact, that I now call myself The Happiness Granny, which I find great fun.

One of the things I've noticed along the way is that people are naturally curious. I know that I have been very curious in exploring the different paths people take to find a better, happier life. I've also discovered that most people would really like an 'Aladdin's lamp' solution, a simple quick fix, preferably administered by someone else, to create the life of their dreams. Remember, Aladdin simply had to rub his magic lamp and out popped a genie to grant his wish.

It took me a long time to realise that all of us already have our own 'genie' within us and this book will show you how to access and direct this amazing power to allow you to enjoy living your own happy and successful life, whatever your dreams.

I now believe I am here to enjoy life and it is with great joy that I sit and write this book. It is important to me to share this with you, with the intention of offering help where help is wanted. Maybe as you read on further, it will strike some chords with you. It is my intention that it will provide you with ideas, information and strategies to explore options and change your life for the better. It is a simple, practical, self-help guide which has the power to inspire you and encourage you to become all that you can be in this life.

Read it with as open a mind as you can and your life will change!

Happiness Is A Way Of Living

I started my introduction by saying that everybody wants to be happy and this is a pre-supposition of how I experience the world and all that I write about in this book. Let me explain what I mean by pre-supposition. It is a concept which is treated as a fundamental principle or idea which underpins the thinking and ideas being expressed. It is something which is taken as being true, because that seems to be an appropriate basis. It doesn't have to be proved true, just accepted as a useful concept. You act as if a pre-supposition were true for you.

Recently I watched a programme on the television where mathematicians were discussing the concept of infinity. Now I'm no mathematician, but I do find the idea of infinity intriguing. Can there really be infinity? What I learned was that, for most mathematicians, infinity is a fiction that was created to help them solve problems. Some say that there can be no such thing as infinity because however big a number you can create, you can always add one to it. It became really interesting when Graham, the mathematician whose name is given to the largest number used by mathematicians, explained that by using the concept of this fictional number they had been able to develop the formulae which enable the internet to function. Even Graham who had created this number can't define it and has no idea how big it really is.

This all gets way beyond me, but my simple understanding from all of this is that it can be very useful, sometimes, to act as if something were true without actually knowing whether or not it is. I know this from my own experience and it's reassuring to have it confirmed by other people who live in a very different reality from mine.

Soon after starting my counselling training, one of my tutors, Rita, who became a good friend, lent me a book which had a profound impact on me and facilitated a huge shift in my awareness. It was called *You Can Heal Your Life* written by Louise Hay.

At that time, I was very caught up in my story about what a miserable childhood I had had. There's nothing unusual about that. Many unhappy people look back to their childhood and put the blame for their current situation back there. I can still see this event clearly. I was sitting on the sofa under the window in my kitchen on a bright, sunny spring day, enjoying reading this book which was so strongly recommended by my friend.

Suddenly, I was so outraged by what I read that I hurled the book across the room in fury. "What rubbish!" I fumed. "How dare she suggest that? She's barmy. I'm not going to read this nonsense!" The book flew across the room as if jet-propelled until it came into contact with the Rayburn stove and crashed on to the floor on the other side of the kitchen.

I was not normally given to such behaviour, so what had prompted this spectacular outburst? I had read Louise's contention that before we are born into this world we exist in the spirit world, and in this place we choose our parents in the life to come. We make an agreement with them so that we can have experiences to help us to learn things we want to learn in this lifetime.

At that time, I was very fixed in a logical, rational, three-dimensional world where if I couldn't understand or explain something, I was very dismissive of it. Just imagine what an affront to my belief systems this was. In the **spirit world!** Nonsense!! **Choose** my parents? I would **never** have chosen them! I was not going to read such tripe and I would let Rita know in no uncertain terms what I thought of this book she had recommended to me!

I fumed and fumed and the book kept going round and round in my head. You know how it is when you hear a song that you really dislike, but there is something catchy about it and you just keep playing it in your head, even though you don't want to. That's what happened with what I had read. Every so often it would pop up again, to my increasing irritation.

Then after a few days I came up with a question that completely changed my perspective. One day, as I stewed in these unpalatable ideas, I suddenly thought: what would happen if I did believe that I chose my parents? I don't, of course, but just suppose I did? What would happen in my life then? I got an immediate answer: well I would just stop blaming my parents and get on with my life as I want it to be. Hmmm. Well, what would happen if I just acted as if I did believe it? I could get on with my life and be happier now. It was one of those life-changing moments that just seem so obvious once they've happened. I felt a huge sense of relief as I decided that I would just act like that anyway.

Then I started changing my focus from blaming all the problems in my life on my past to focusing on how I want my life to be and creating what I want.

Several years later, when I began training in the wonderful world of NLP, I learned that what I had done in choosing to take something as if it were true is known as using a pre-supposition. NLP stands for Neuro Linguistic Programming and explores the relationships between how we think (neuro), how we communicate (linguistic) and the patterns of behaviour and emotions we create (programming). It provides methodology for exploring and understanding how humans operate and how we can quickly and easily make changes in our lives.

It was started in the 1970s by two Americans: Richard Bandler, a mathematician, and John Grinder, a linguist. They wanted to find out what it is that makes some people outstanding in what they do – exactly how they create excellence in their lives. I was given the definition of NLP as being 'the study of the structure of subjective experience' – how people create their unique experience of the world.

In NLP a pre-supposition is something you have 'supposed' to be true. It doesn't matter whether or not it actually is true, you just act as if it is true because that will be beneficial to you, just as taking the concept of choosing my parents was useful for me. I couldn't prove it one way or the other, but when I chose to act as if it were true, I became happier.

You are unique

Every individual on the planet is unique. No matter how many similarities you have with other people, no one else is exactly the same as you. You are unique and your uniqueness is your gift to the world, what you are bringing to the party. That's the 'what'. NLP focuses on the 'how'. How you create the 'what'. How you use your mind and experiences to create the 'you'.

NLP offers very practical, powerful strategies for facilitating understanding and change in any area of your life, often amazingly quickly and easily. In NLP we use pre-suppositions and I would like to offer you some pre-suppositions now:

- ♥ *You are much, much more than you think you are*
- ♥ *All reality is a construction*
- ♥ *Every behaviour has a positive intention*

♥ *Living is a continuous process of learning*
♥ *Everyone and everything is interconnected*

I invite you to consider these as I expand on them a little. They are useful to me in my life and to my clients in theirs. As you consider them, hold the possibility that they could in some way be useful to you.

You are much, much more than you think you are

Many people have a habit of playing small and thinking about themselves in a very limited way.

"Oh, I'm just a small cog… just a housewife… just one of six billion people on this planet, just a…."

Even those who, by most people's standards, are doing very well in life, will often compare themselves unfavourably with others. It's a common trait amongst we humans to restrict our thinking. There is so much more going on in this world than you can appreciate or comprehend and you are part of all this, although you may not yet appreciate how.

Could it be that you have all the resources you need to start to create whatever your heart desires? How would your life be if you took that one on?

All reality is a construction

There is no such thing as objective reality. Scientists have now discovered that even the most carefully constructed experiments are influenced by the expectations of the people carrying them out and that so-called random processes can actually be influenced by thought.

What you think of as reality is simply your perception, a map you have created. It is not the 'territory' you are describing. Just ask any police officer about witness statements. They will tell you how people will genuinely swear to having witnessed details of an event which conflict with other genuine people's statements. All are absolutely convinced that their version is true.

Or think of a time when you and someone else had different recollections of an event or situation. For example, when you have been reminiscing with a friend, remembering a particular occasion you both enjoyed and you find that you don't agree about what happened, or who said, or did, what. Both of you are right, according to your reality.

Look at this image. What do you see? Is it a duck or is it a rabbit or is it something else? I like ducks and don't much care for rabbits and so I first saw it as a duck. What do you see? Play with changing it from one to the other. Both are true.

At some time, you may have encountered people who didn't appreciate your views and told you something like "get real" or "face reality." What they really meant was "change to my reality." Your reality is your reality which you have constructed and in this book we will explore how you do this and how you can do this to intentionally create the life your heart desires.

Every behaviour has a positive intention

People are always doing the best they can with the skills, knowledge and experience they have available to them at the time. They choose what to them seems to be the best option. To an onlooker it may appear unacceptable, antisocial, bizarre, or in some way inappropriate, but an onlooker cannot know exactly what has led that person to think and behave that way.

If you think about your own life, you may come up with some examples of things you have done in the past which you might feel uncomfortable about now. You think that if you were in a similar situation now, you would do things differently. But at the time you did what seemed right for you. When we know better, we do better. You made the best choice you could at the time.

Living is a continuous process of learning

Whatever you think about what you are doing living here on earth now, whether you have a mission or life purpose, or maybe you don't think about such things, one thing perhaps you could agree is that everything we do gives us an opportunity to learn. A favourite NLP saying is that there is no such thing as failure, only feedback. I remember hearing a very skilful counsellor saying to a young lad, "It was a very good idea – it just didn't work out the way you wanted it to. Now what could you do?"

That was so much more empowering for the boy than the negative, critical comments he was used to hearing. He moved from being embarrassed and dejected about a 'problem' to feeling empowered to go back and make another attempt to deal with a situation.

Thomas Edison, who invented the light bulb, made over five thousand attempts to create it. He knew that there is no such thing as failure, only feedback, and is quoted as saying that he found many ways for it not to work before he finally found the way which did work. Most people would have given up and think that they had failed. He, however, knew he was on to something and he kept going until it worked. You can never learn less and everything in your life is an opportunity for you to learn.

Everyone and everything is interconnected

Mystics and spiritual teachers have taught for centuries that we are one, that we are all part of the same creative energy. Scientists now talk about a unified field which connects everyone and everything in existence. Everyone and everything in this wonderfully varied world is made up of the same basic building blocks. We are all made of the same stuff, it's just organised differently.

You are constantly influencing and being influenced by many others and are mostly unaware of this happening. It is now said that you are only six steps of connection away from any other person in the world – you know someone, who knows someone, who knows someone... and in six steps you will connect with them. You are more connected than you think.

So, having started to consider these pre-suppositions, how many do you think you might be willing to experiment with and practise as useful now?

Happiness

I started this chapter by saying that everybody wants to be happy. So what am I talking about? My pocket Oxford dictionary defines happy as 'feeling or showing pleasure or contentment, fortunate'. In my many years of working with people, I have yet to find anyone who does not want this, or more of this in their life and over the years I have helped many, many people to adapt their thinking and behaviour to achieve this.

Sometimes it has been just a simple shift in their perception, one simple idea that sparked their awareness of the happiness that is available to them – this duck could be a rabbit. Sometimes, it has been a longer, slower process and this doesn't matter. Whether it's an instant Eureka! moment or whether it's a slower awakening is irrelevant. Remember, everyone is unique and will create their own experience of becoming happier. The bottom line is that anyone who wants to be happier can be, whatever their circumstances.

Happiness is an attitude, a way of living, as one of my neighbours taught me a few years ago. We had recently moved into a new home and were busy re-creating a vegetable garden from an overgrown plot. I put in many, many hours during that first spring and summer and there was a lot of hard graft involved. Over the months, I got to know my next door neighbour, Vera, a lady in her nineties, who lived in a little cottage with a garden adjoining ours.

Often, I would be working away when she would appear at the wall. She was always bright and cheerful. She would make encouraging comments about the progress I was making and tell me how much she was enjoying seeing the garden take shape. I noticed that every conversation we had ended with the words, "Bless your heart."

I also noticed that in our many conversations she never complained, never ever. What a refreshing change it was to talk with her, as she was always very happy and appreciative of life. Although other people told me about her history and past sadness in her life, in conversations with me she was always happy in the present. Even when she appeared one day with a bandaged arm after being knocked over and bitten by a dog, all she said was, "Well it was a shock, but it's going on all right now."

The day I dug the first new potatoes and pulled the first carrots and shared them with her, she was almost ecstatic and bubbling over with appreciation as she was holding them, admiring them and anticipating eating them later. It was such a joy to share her delight in something so simple but so meaningful to her, and I got my heart blessed a lot that day!

When Vera passed away peacefully in her sleep one night, my sadness was greatly outweighed by my appreciation for what she had taught me, in demonstrating how to live happily. She had developed happiness as an attitude and a way of living, whatever the world brought to her, and was much loved by many and a great inspiration to me, bless her heart.

Over the years, I have noticed that some people like to trivialise and underestimate the importance of happiness and aim for what they think are more lofty goals, such as fulfilment and particular achievements. I noticed a headline to an article recently in which a television personality (why do we pay so much attention to them?) stated that she didn't want her daughter to be happy, she wanted her to be fulfilled. Well, in my book, literally, she will never be fulfilled unless she is happy. Happiness is fundamental to well-being. It is contradictory to suggest that you can experience well-being without underlying happiness.

As I said earlier, this book is about simple practical aspects of living. So, if you are wanting changes in your life, start by paying attention to being happy.

Many years ago, I was intrigued to read of the kingdom of Bhutan, a tiny country in the Himalayas which doesn't measure the success of its country by its Gross Domestic Product, or Gross National Product (measures of the financial value of a country's economy) as western countries do, but, instead, by Gross National Happiness. What a wonderful concept! Although I don't normally take much interest in politics, I am delighted that our government in the UK is now taking an interest in people's level of happiness and has just carried out the first survey. This could lead to some very interesting and beneficial policies.

In April 2012, delegates at a landmark United Nations meeting, convened by representatives of Bhutan, proposed making well-being the central goal of economic development. In effect, they were calling for a happiness-based economy. The Prime Minister of Bhutan describes happiness not as an everyday passing mood, but the deep abiding happiness that comes from living in harmony and feeling totally connected with our world. That makes perfect sense to me.

How happy are you?

Now we get to the question: How happy are you? Maybe this is a question you frequently ask yourself or maybe, like most people in our busy, busy lives, it's not something you usually stop to consider. Stop now and in a moment put the book down and consider.

On a scale of nought to ten, with nought being absolute zero and ten being as much as you can imagine, give yourself a score for the whole of your life as it is right now. Just do this quickly. Ask yourself the question and make a note of the first number that pops into your mind. Ask yourself:

"How happy am I?"

Now get a sheet of paper and a pen and take two or three minutes, or more if you want, to make a list of what makes you happy in life, or what you think would make you happy.

One of my favourite NLP trainers is an American called Topher Morrison. When I heard that he was leading a seminar called *The Mental Game of Life*, I went along for some fun. It was great fun and very entertaining. Then at one point Topher said words to the effect of, "If you want to be happy, it's simple. Lower your standards." 'WHAT?' my inner voice screamed. Most motivational speakers exhort people to 'raise your game' and 'aim for more' etc. What does he mean 'lower your standards'?

Then the penny dropped. Vera had taught me the value of finding happiness in small everyday things. My study and experience of the law of attraction had taught me that if there is something you want, the more you focus on the area in which you already have some of it, the more of it you will attract into your life.

What many people don't realise is that they have things the wrong way round. They think of things outside their current experience and, encouraged by the media, marketing and current 'celebrity culture', brainwash themselves into believing they can only be happy if they have the highly successful job, flash car, fabulous home, perfect partner, millions in the bank, a holiday home as well, perfect teeth, etc., etc. The list goes on and the important aspect of this is the belief that happiness can only be achieved when they have these external things, which are outside their current experience.

Maybe this is exaggerated or maybe you think that you don't do this. However, I imagine you can relate to this to some extent. It's human nature to want things. It's simply part of the creative energy of the universe. You are a unique expression of this energy and it is natural for you to have desires. This is how the universe expands. I know this is contrary to some religious and cultural doctrines which insist that desires are 'bad' and must be cast aside. Well, most doctrines contain some unhelpful elements and are only true for you if you believe them to be so. Desires are perfectly natural.

It makes more sense to me to believe or follow guidance that acknowledges what a wonderfully unique expression of the creative flow your life is and that you have all the resources you need to create the life you want now. Remember, whatever you think you are, you are much, much more than that.

Little things that make you happy

With Vera in mind, take up your list again and now start to add all the little things in life that make you happy – all those little things that maybe you take for granted in your everyday life, without noticing how happy they make you, because your focus is on something outside your everyday life, which you perceive as being lacking.

My list of little things that make me happy includes walking hand in hand with Terence, Marmite, a hug from a grandson, someone smiling at me, watching birds on the bird table in my garden, my very comfortable walking boots, sitting in front of a log fire....

Now write your list of what makes you happy. Keep this list handy and add to it when you think of something else. The longer your list gets, the better life gets. It's easy to overlook all the little everyday happy happenings until you realise how important they are and how they create the foundation of your overall happiness. Then, by noticing what you already have, you can create more.

Celebrate all the happy things in your life now

You may already be familiar with the saying that you get more of what you give your attention to. So play with this and the experience of happiness if you want to be happier (and I can't believe that there is anyone who wouldn't want to be). However happy you are, there is always space for more. The more happiness you are experiencing in your life now, the more you will create.

Many people trundle along with mantras such as 'it's not too bad', 'mustn't grumble', 'it could be worse' and inadvertently deny themselves a wonderfully happy and, consequently, fulfilling life. You are here to live a life which has the potential to fulfil all of your heart's desires.

Roko Belic, director of the film *Happy*, tells us that happy people enjoy better health, longer lives, more creativity and are more law-abiding and caring for their environment. He sums up with: "Increasing happiness brings big benefits for individuals, communities and society as a whole." So who wouldn't want to be happy?

Imagine happiness becoming a way of living for you

Make it your intention, make it a game, make it a treasure hunt, get creative and start noticing all the expressions and nuances of happiness in your daily life. Just imagine being ecstatically happy about your equivalent of a handful of new potatoes.

There is a saying, 'If you do what you've always done, you'll get what you've always got'. Einstein's definition of insanity is 'repeatedly doing the same things and expecting to get a different result'. In addition to reading this book, you will start doing things differently or doing different things. This may be a deliberate choice or you may just notice that things are changing. Either way is better, depending on your perception.

At the end of each day make a note of at least three things which you have noticed feeling happy about today and when you go to bed, as you are relaxing just before you go to sleep, start wondering about the happy things in store for you tomorrow.

Just the happy things you
are lining up....

CHAPTER TWO

You Create The Life You Are Living

And when you wake up the next morning, while you're still in that relaxed state as you are returning to this conscious awareness, repeat the process and start imagining all the good things which might come your way today. Maybe, like many people, as you wake up your mind immediately focuses on something less than pleasant that you are expecting today. 'Oh, no, I've got that meeting with that difficult customer, that report to finish by 10.00 a.m., fifty things to do and only an hour to do them', and so on. You think of all the 'problems' and 'difficulties' you have lined up.

Now is the time to start changing that and begin by thinking of pleasant options which uplift and inspire you before you get up and begin your day.

Appreciate your uniqueness

You are unique. There is no one else in this world who is exactly the same as you. In the six billion plus people of this world you are the only one of you. Even so-called identical twins do, in fact, have some differences.

So you are the only you and you are creating the reality of your life. Later we will be looking at how you do this, but right now I would like you to consider and appreciate your uniqueness.

Right now start thinking about you and what you are uniquely bringing to this world. No one else has exactly the same combination of life experiences, education, DNA, understanding, opinions, skills and talents, ideas and aspirations that you have.

I invite you to start acknowledging and even celebrating your uniqueness in the spirit of appreciation. You are a beautiful being. You are amazing way beyond your current imagination. Please appreciate this.

Our deepest fear

You may already be familiar with spiritual teacher Marianne Williamson's much-repeated quotation which begins:

'Our deepest fear is not that we are inadequate. Our deepest fear is that we are powerful beyond measure. It is our light, not our darkness that most frightens us.'

What if that were true for you? However successful you are in your life, are there areas where you are playing smaller than you would really like to and not letting your beautiful light shine as fully as you could? Maybe now is the time for you to let your genie out and allow yourself to become who you really want to be.

Your conscious mind and your unconscious mind

In order to understand how you create your life, you need to be more aware of how your minds work. There are two aspects of the mind to consider here: the conscious mind and the unconscious mind.

In your busy, busy world you are constantly bombarded with information which comes through your senses. You see, hear, feel, taste, smell and just sense/experience what is going on.

Imagine you are walking down a street. You are managing your body, keeping yourself walking. At the same time, you are interacting with other people walking along the street and with the traffic on the road. You see lots of adverts and colourful shop windows. You go into a shop. Maybe there's something specific you are looking for. You see even more displays, advertising materials, hear broadcast messages about special offers, notice your new shoe is rubbing your heel, see someone you know – always more and more information for you to deal with.

So how does your mind cope? One way of making sense of what we do is to use the model of the mind having two parts: the conscious mind and the unconscious mind. In this model, the conscious mind is the part which thinks it is in charge, which defines your present awareness. It is logical, rational and orderly.

The unconscious mind is the 'storeroom' for all your experiences – everything you have ever done, said, thought, imagined, heard, seen etc. – everything gets stored here. What a mind-blowing idea! It gets better – this wonderful unconscious mind takes everything literally, operates in a similar way to a five-year-old and really is in charge, but doesn't know it is. If you often find your or other people's behaviour surprising or hard to fathom, perhaps this awareness is shedding some light on things.

Years ago, I learned that your brain receives 2.3 million bits of information per second. Can you imagine that? It's huge. Whatever the exact figures are, there is an immense amount of information being received by your brain and most of it is being handled on autopilot, without you consciously knowing about it. All this information is processed in the unconscious mind, which passes information to the conscious mind.

In 1956, Professor George A Miller of Harvard University published his conclusion that the conscious mind, the part of the mind that is 'noticing' what you are experiencing, thus creating your present awareness, can hold or notice seven, plus or minus two, bits of information at any one time. That means between five and nine bits of information. Current research at Oxford University has reduced this number to 2.8 bits at any one time.

This diagram is a simple representation of the relationship between the capacity of the conscious mind (the dot in the middle) and the unconscious mind (the shaded area).

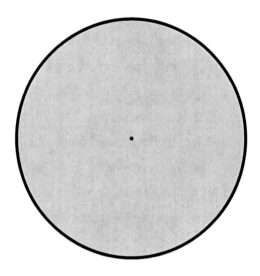

The dot in the centre of the circle is your conscious mind with its seven, plus or minus two, bits of information per second and the rest of the circle is your unconscious mind, with its 2.3 million plus bits of information per second, reminding you that you are much, much more than you think and that you have all these resources available to you.

The main purpose of your unconscious mind is to keep you safe and maintain your well-being. From this vast reservoir of information, 'selected' information passes into the present awareness of the conscious mind.

Your unconscious mind holds information about everything that has ever happened to you in your life and it constantly oversees your experience of events, which can be divided into five areas: body, emotions, memory, performance and communication.

Your body is run by your unconscious mind so that it seems as if things happen automatically. You don't have to tell your heart to beat, or your lungs to breathe or if you want to turn a page, you don't have to go through the process of instructing every muscle in sequence to direct this action. You do all of these and most of your everyday actions without thinking. Your unconscious mind takes care of it, operating on the principle of least effort.

The unconscious mind is also the domain of that whole range of emotions you experience. It also takes everything personally and is a highly moral being.

All of your memories of all that has ever happened to you, all that you have ever experienced, are organised and stored in your unconscious mind. Painful or unpleasant memories may be repressed to protect you and sometimes may be delivered up to your conscious mind for confirmation to support current thinking.

Your performance is governed by your unconscious mind which functions best as a whole, maintains instincts, needs repetition and is programmed to seek. It's always on the lookout. It's your twenty-four/seven bodyguard.

All of your communication is directed by your unconscious mind, since it determines how you perceive events and experiences. It often expresses symbolically, takes things literally and does not process 'not'. There is more information about the functioning of the unconscious mind and the NLP communication model in Chapter Six.

You give your life meaning

As you are creating your life, you give your life meaning. You are the one living your life, having the experiences of living on this planet at this time, in your particular circumstances. However much, or little, you are consciously influenced by others, you will create your unique set of beliefs and draw your own conclusions about how life is for you. You tell your own story. You are continuously creating your story and your story becomes the life you live.

Life is constantly changing in many ways. That's how it is. You could never stand still even if you wanted to. Just look at modern technology, for example. Who would have imagined, even a few years ago, that with a small mobile phone, not much bigger than a credit card, we could call up someone anywhere in the world and see them on screen as we talk with them? This used to be the stuff of science fiction. Now it's everyday reality for millions of people. You're probably ahead of me on this. I've only just got round to having a mobile phone.

As these changes go on all around, you have the choice to embrace them or resist them, but one thing is certain: change will continue. We live in an expanding universe.

Terence and I resisted what we saw as the curse of the mobile phone until it became too uncomfortable being so out of step with most of the people we know. They couldn't believe that we were not contactable at all times, or that they couldn't text us. So now we're letting life become easier for ourselves and telling a slightly different story. We've let go of thinking we're right in maintaining that mobile phones are intrusive, a nuisance and add to the stresses of modern living. Instead we're embracing the idea that they can be very useful, making contact with others easier and, of course, we can turn them off when we choose to be unavailable.

We haven't quite embraced texting yet, but maybe we'll get there soon.

Your current story directs your future

So everyone creates their own story of their life. You are creating your story and the story you tell right now directs your future. If you want to create a different future in which you are happier, healthier, more successful, or whatever it is you want, then start telling a different story, one which feels better.

However attached you are to the story you have created about your life and why it is the way it is, or why you haven't been able to do or have or be what you wanted to, you can, if you're willing, create a different perspective. People get attached to their story and think it's right and close their mind to how unhappy this makes them.

Would you rather be right or be happy?

A lovely lady called Iris came to see me. She had advanced cancer and came for some healing and kindness. She was in her fifties and as she walked slowly into my therapy room I noticed a very strong smell of rotting flesh. The cancer was ulcerating and I felt nauseous as

I approached her. I couldn't imagine what it was like for her living with that stomach-churning smell literally under her nose all day.

Iris received some Reiki healing which relieved her physical discomfort and we talked about her life. She told me that for several years she had been caught up in a battle with a lawyer whom she believed had acted in a way that had created major problems in her life. She was totally focused on how he had wronged her and ruined her life, as she saw things, and she was determined that he should be made to pay for his negligence and incompetence. She had spent years and most of her money going from lawyer to lawyer trying to find someone who could make him pay. By the time she came to see me, her body was becoming very frail and she was living in a cold house with buckets to catch the water from the leaking roof.

She came to see me five times and always felt some relief of her pain. We talked about what she was creating in her life, which she acknowledged. She described her hostility towards the lawyer as "eating away at me", but it was a matter of principle for her and she was adamant that this terrible man must pay for the wrong he had done. The last time I saw Iris, as she left she calmly said, "I know that holding on to this fight is killing me, but I can't let go." She was right, bless her heart.

"If you had to choose, would you rather be right or be happy?" is a very powerful question to ask yourself.

I wonder what story you tell and what meanings you give to your life. It is part of human nature to search for meaning and understanding. We are naturally curious creatures. I spent many years believing that life was a struggle and I had to work hard and put in a lot of effort to achieve anything. That didn't make me very happy or nice to be around.

I now choose to believe that life is a game and the more lightly I can hold this belief, the more enjoyable life is. The more I am enjoying life, the more pleasant I am to be with and the kinder I am. The kinder I am, the more of a beneficial presence I am here in this world and that's what I want to be.

How do you see life?

You may believe that you are here with a specific purpose or calling. I recently met Sara, who is a very inspiring professional in the education world. By the age of ten she knew that she wanted to be a teacher. She could already see herself as a teacher and just couldn't imagine doing anything else. She just 'knew' she was going to be a teacher. As she told me this, she held out her hands, fingers pointing forwards, palms parallel about four inches apart, saying that she could see it like a train track. That was what she was going to do and that was where she was going.

Sara went off to university and when it was time to get a job she saw one advertised in a special educational needs setting. At that time she didn't have any specific qualifications or experience in this area, but felt very strongly that this was the area where she wanted to work. To her surprise and delight, she got the job and now, fifteen years later, is still at the same school, totally committed to her work and loving it.

As she spoke to me, her eyes shone, she was very animated and it was obvious that she was very passionate about helping her teenage pupils to develop their skills and talents in spite of their perceived limitations. She just can't imagine doing anything else with her life and is a marvellous champion for her pupils. When I listened to her I found her passion and enthusiasm very inspiring.

It doesn't really matter what you believe or what meaning you give to your life. What really matters is what this philosophy leads you to do or be in this world and ultimately how happy you are. As I said in the last chapter, you have more resources available to you than you realise, including your genie. Remember, you are much, much more than you think you are and what you think ultimately creates who you are and how you experience life.

You are a unique, talented person who may or may not yet be developing or appreciating some of the talents you actually have. You can if you wish treat this world as a wonderful playground with lots of fun activities and experiences on offer. Just imagine what adventures you could have and who you would play with.

You may see it as a wonderful banquet laid out before you, an amazing buffet offering all kinds of delicious, exotic, familiar and unfamiliar foods from all around the world. All you have to do is pick up a plate and help yourself.

This world, however you currently view it, is filled with wonderful opportunities and no one else can experience them for you. Everywhere you look there are opportunities. Start noticing what else is on offer beyond the self-created boundaries that your lovely conscious mind sets up for you.

Mistaken beliefs

It's as if you have forgotten some aspects of who you really are. You have become conditioned, maybe by external influences or maybe by your own limiting beliefs. In my counselling training, which was based on the work of Alfred Adler, a colleague of Freud and Jung but with a philosophy that was much more palatable for me, I was introduced to the concept of 'mistaken beliefs'. These are beliefs which we form, often as young children, based on the information and understanding we have at the time. We are told things by the adults around us. We experience things with a limited understanding of the world and draw conclusions based on our personal perceptions.

We create beliefs which we carry through life, often just taking them for granted as truth because we have believed them for a long time. When you realise that it was just a mistaken belief and it is perfectly understandable that you took this on at the time, you are free to create new beliefs which are more appropriate for the life you are living now and the life you wish to create.

You are an innately creative person

In my model of the world, you are part of the creative expansion of the universe and you are here to create. If you have limited yourself by denying your creative nature or have not yet allowed yourself to explore this, well now you can.

Bandler and Grinder, the founders of NLP, wanted to discover how people created excellence in their lives so that this could be taught and replicated by others. I believe you might as well create excellence in your life. You are here spending your time, living your life and I wonder how much happier you would be knowing you are creating excellence in your life, whatever that would be for you.

How would it be if you stopped playing safe to the extent that you usually do? What if you stopped settling for the familiar and the known and shook off the conditioning that limits the wonderfully expansive creative person you could be, creating excellence in your life now?

Here is a simple NLP breakdown of the process of creating excellence:

The 4 Steps to Creating Excellence in Your Life

1. *Know what you want*

First you think of something that you want and I suggest you start with something that you consider do-able, that's not too far from your current experience. It's a good strategy to build your creating muscles with 'small' exercises to start with and as you get the confidence in your ability to consciously create, you will automatically expand your goals.

2. *Be flexible*

If you wish to create something new in your life, you have to be willing to be flexible in your thinking and behaviour. You know that if you do what you've always done you will get what you've always got and so it's logical that you will need to change some aspects of what you usually think and do.

3. *Use your senses with precision*

That means notice what feedback you are getting. Pay careful attention to what you are seeing, hearing and feeling.

4. Take action now

You may call this informed action or inspired action. It's what you do after noticing the feedback you're getting from all of your senses. Many people know that they have to take action to get results and run around like headless chickens taking random action. With inspired action you will 'sense' what action to take and when.

These four simple steps will lead you to creating excellence in your life now, whatever it is you choose to create.

CHAPTER THREE

Keep It Simple

When I told my friend Fay that the chapter I had just written was called Keep It Simple, she asked, "So, are you just going to put a smiley face on the page and leave it at that?" Since I'd already written the rest, I decided to keep it and add the smile, which is now the short version of this chapter.

More, more, more, faster, faster, faster

Life is often a juggling act, a balancing act. These days you would have to live in a cave, or in a remote community somewhere far removed from our western so-called civilization, to be unaware of the 'more, more, more, faster, faster, faster' culture that we live in here. We get busier and busier and then create stress and 'problems' for ourselves by having so many balls in the air that it becomes a struggle to keep everything flowing in a balanced way.

We live in a society which buys into the myth that more is better and become hypnotised by the desirability of more-ness. It's all around, everywhere you look and it's so easy to get caught up, swept along and to literally buy into this. We are bombarded by advertising and marketing which very skilfully convinces us that to have a better life we need the latest plasma screen television or the 'smartest' mobile phone or this wonderful processed food which saves so much time.

'More creates happiness' seems to be a common mantra and we buy into it. All will be well in my life if I acquire the latest bright, shiny object – or so the compelling advertising and promotion insists. But is this true? Of course it isn't, but we are so busy, running ourselves ragged trying to be the impossibly perfect person promoted by the advertisers as who we need to be, the one who juggles seventy-five balls and does everything perfectly, that we don't see this. Consequently, a lot of people make themselves very unhappy, and often ill, trying to live up to this myth.

Even if you manage to some extent to remove yourself from this busy-ness, you may then buy into the idea that there could be more to your life by having these things and you're missing something important among all these amazing things on offer. This is just part of being human. You naturally have desires – always have, always will. It's not the actual desires that are important, it's how you act upon them and which ones you choose to follow to create what you want in your life.

Keep it simple

So, how can you become immune to the persuasive powers of the media, the advertisers, your peers who have bought into the myth and want you to join them? A very helpful mantra for you to practise is 'Keep it simple'. A mantra is simply a phrase or sentence you repeat over and over to calm your mind and help you to focus. Or if you don't like the word mantra, you can just call it a strategy and remember to remind yourself of your strategy to keep it simple.

This applies to whatever it is you are dealing with. Have you noticed how human minds love to make things complex when they don't need to be? I don't know whether they're just trying to show how clever they are that they can understand something this complicated. Of course, some things really are complex, but in everyday life people often make things unnecessarily complicated. I get a bit argumentative sometimes when I hear someone telling me this is complex, blah, blah, and think to myself: It doesn't have to be. Is it really? How can it be simple instead?

Sometimes if I ask Terence, who is an engineer, what I think is a simple question, such as, "How do I do...?" he, bless him, may launch into a long explanation. He will tell me what this bit does and how it interacts with that bit and what happens over here and on and on, until eventually, as I wade through all this information, the penny drops and I confirm, "So I just set it on number two?" "Yes." "Thank you. That's the simple answer I was looking for."

My eyes glaze over whenever I hear someone start with something like, "Ah well, you see, what happens is..." because I know I'm in for a long, convoluted or detailed explanation. Please, please keep it simple!

Take a few moments now to consider how busy, busy your life seems to be. How does it feel? Does it feel as though you have plenty of time and space to just be you? Some people think they are extremely busy, running round and round, jumping from one activity to another without any clear plan or structure and not actually achieving very much that's useful, just feelings of exhaustion and being overwhelmed.

We have a long-running joke in my family about the coalman coming. My mother-in-law, in her later years, would ring up to tell us how busy she was because she had the coalman coming the following week and she had to clear up and get ready for him. She had to rake the coal dust to the side of the shed, which in her mind became a huge task and dominated her life for at least a week. We used to find this very amusing and whenever we realise we're making a big deal about some minor upcoming event or activity, we refer to having the coalman coming.

Identify your values

How simple are you letting your life be? One thing that can help with this is to identify your values in life and make sure you are living them. Your values are, literally, what you value in life, what is most important to you. It may be that you value your career above all else. It may be money or freedom or health, or whatever you have decided is important to you.

A high-powered, high-earning banker probably has little appreciation of a hippy lifestyle and vice versa.

Neither is right nor wrong, just different according to their values. You are unique and create your own value system. Life becomes more simple when you are clear about your values. How much you are living in alignment with your values affects how happy you are in life. Often people think they value something very highly but get caught up in situations or a career or lifestyle which is at odds with their values.

A common story is of the high-achieving business person who has spent so much time focusing on their work that they have neglected their relationships or family life. One day their spouse says they want a divorce and their family life is gone. The career was originally the means to provide for the family but became the priority, and eventually the family life was lost.

I grew up on a farm in the Cotswolds where I had lots of freedom in open countryside and ponies to ride so that I could roam at will, which was wonderful. Freedom is still high on my list of values, which supports my passion for helping people to become aware of how much freedom of choice they really have in their lives, whatever they are used to thinking.

To become aware of the values in your life, take a sheet of paper and a pen and ask yourself:

"What is important in my life?"

Write down whatever comes to mind and then ask:

"What else is important?"

Write it down and then ask:

"And what else is important?"

Think about your life and keep going with "And what else is important?" until you really have nothing to add. Allow yourself about ten minutes for this and just keep going until you are sure you have finished. Sometimes really important values pop out way down the list and so it's helpful to keep going and give yourself plenty of time to do this.

Take a short break when you've finished. Then come back to your list and start to evaluate it. Look at all the words on your list and rank them in order of importance, from one to ten, so that you come up with a list of your top ten values, or values hierarchy as it is called.

This provides you with very useful information to support you in consciously creating the life you want. If your current lifestyle is out of sync with your values, then you won't be very happy. It's as simple as that.

If there is something you really want in your life, then it, or the value which represents it, needs to appear high up on your list. The higher it is on your list, the more importance you are giving it. So if there's something you want which is appearing towards the bottom of your list, you need to pay more attention to it and move it up the list.

A common example of this is money. A person wants more money in their life but they have conflicting beliefs or ideas about money. They may buy into the 'money is the root of all evil' nonsense, or the 'mustn't be greedy' mentality or some other thinking which deters them from giving favourable attention to money. Like everything else in this world, money is simply energy and energy flows where attention goes. Energy needs to flow and so does money.

Have you noticed what people who have lots of money talk about? They're happy to talk about money. Have you noticed what people who are hard up talk about? They tend to bang on about being hard up. So a person who wants more money in their life can appreciate the money they do already have and pay it more attention, to move it up their values list. There is a saying, 'What you appreciate, appreciates' Practise it with money if you want to have more in your life.

Check your list and see how well your values hierarchy corresponds to what you want in your life and be open to making any necessary changes. Having access to clear information is part of keeping things simple.

How is your life rolling along?

My question for you now is, "How is your life rolling along? Is it rolling smoothly or are you having a bumpy ride?"

For this next piece of information gathering, you will need a sheet of paper and a pen or some crayons or coloured pens if you're feeling creative and want to brighten things up.

To keep things simple, this exercise divides your life into six main areas: health/well-being, recreation/social life, relationships/family, work/career, money and personal/spiritual development. For a happy, smoothly running life, it's very important that you give enough attention to all of these areas.

Your Life Wheel

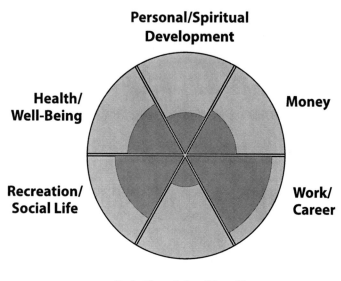

Personal/Spiritual Development

Health/ Well-Being

Money

Recreation/ Social Life

Work/ Career

Relationships/Family

On your sheet of paper make a copy of the outline of this life wheel (without the shading) and then:

1. *Look at one area and ask yourself, "On a scale of nought to ten, how happy am I about this area of my life?" Just go with whatever number pops into your mind.*

2. *Then, designating the hub of the wheel as nought and the outer rim as ten, draw a line across the 'spokes' of this area to represent the number you have given it.*

3. *Shade or colour the central part of this area.*

4. *Do this for each area in turn and discover how balanced a life wheel you are creating.*

This will give you a very graphic representation of your current lifestyle and will highlight for you areas which need more attention. It may surprise you. It may even shock you. If your wheel shows a wide range of scores, like the example above, you can understand now why your life sometimes feels uncomfortable. You are giving yourself a bumpy ride.

The first time I did this, it showed me that I really had been neglecting my health and physical well-being. I was so caught up in head stuff that I was overlooking my health. Once I saw this I was able to address it. I didn't need to take drastic action or make major changes, just start taking a bit more exercise and a bit more care about what I ate. When I scored the wheel again a few months later, it was much more balanced.

Be kind to yourself

Whatever information you get, be kind to yourself. This is most important. Actually, it's important in everything you do, but especially so here. You have been doing the best you could with all the skills, knowledge and information available to you. Now that you have more information you can use this to develop your current thinking and behaviour. See it as a game to get your wheel rolling smoothly and, as it becomes smoother, you will also automatically expand all areas so that your overall happiness increases.

Ask for help

Remember that you are a creative person and can have fun creating your life the way you want it. Maybe you know what you need to do to improve things and can get started straight away. Many people are reluctant to ask for help, but if you need help with improving any area of your wheel, then ask for it. You can start by looking online or in the library. There is a wealth of free information available. Go to a professional who specialises in the area you wish to address: if your finances are a mess, for example, consult someone who is an expert on financial management; if you have health issues, consult a healthcare expert. You need more information and there are plenty of places you can get it. It's very simple: you just have to be willing to ask for help.

You will find that once you decide to pay more attention to an area, you will start to notice how often related information comes into your awareness. There is a part of your brain called the reticular activating system which brings to your attention things that are currently of interest to you, or that you have decided to give more attention to.

No doubt you have had an experience where you are considering buying, or have just bought, a new gadget, toy or item of some sort which you thought was something really special. Suddenly it's as if everywhere you go, it's there. You pick up a newspaper and see an advert for it or notice a review for it. You see it on the television, you discover your neighbour has just got one, etc., etc. Before your particular interest, all this information would have passed you by in the millions of bits of information coming your way. Now it is meaningful to you and comes into your conscious awareness.

Many years ago, Terence and I were thinking of buying a new car. We were very excited to be buying our first brand new car and we spent ages choosing the model of car and studying the colour chart before picking what we thought was a very smart shade of red. We hadn't seen this model of car in this colour before and we thought it looked really special. Once we had ordered the car we began to notice cars in the same shade as ours. Then, as we started driving around in our lovely new car, we realised how many there actually were on the roads. Of course, they were there before we bought ours but had no relevance to us. At the time we were less than impressed with this discovery.

Using the life wheel is one of the best and easiest ways I know to get an awareness, a picture, of what you are creating and start considering what changes in focus you might want to start making. A calm approach to this is the most productive. Often people decide to make drastic changes to 'really sort their life out' once and for all, in a way that turns out to be unachievable for them and so is counterproductive. Instead of improving things, they just end up giving up and feeling worse about themselves and their life.

New Year's resolutions are a great example of this. Have you ever set yourself a big goal which very quickly crashed and burned? You got all fired up in the comfort of your armchair. Yes, you were really going to do it this time: lose that two stone which had taken up residence in your body, because you'd seen this amazing Gobble It diet which people were raving about; or run the London marathon this year, because you'd seen that you can get fit enough to run a marathon in only six weeks; or get an Open University degree to improve your career prospects and you only have to study for twenty hours a week. It's going to be great, you tell yourself.

No, it probably isn't. It's too far removed from your normal experience. Did you know that three quarters of people who, in a fit of wild optimism, take out an annual subscription at a gym or health club never actually use it more than once or twice?

So before making decisions about drastic changes to your life, remember to be kind to yourself and develop a longer term, more achievable approach to creating the life you want. Start with small steps to build your conscious creating muscles and confidence. I know it's understandable in our 'now,

now, now, instant gratification' culture, supported by advertisers' and marketers' outrageous promises, to want it all today.

However, you might be amazed at how making smaller, easier changes actually impacts your overall sense of well-being far more than you would have expected. Go with what feels do-able now, rather than what you want to think you could perhaps do.

A good place to start is by reducing your overall busy-ness. Take a look at the areas in your life where you feel most pressured, or overwhelmed even. Practise asking yourself 'Keep It Simple' questions such as:

- ♥ *"Do I really want or need to do this?"*
- ♥ *"Is now the best time to do this?"*
- ♥ *"How can I let this situation or task be simpler?"*

Start looking for and asking for ways to let your life be simple, wherever you are and whatever you are doing.

Let simple be easy

"Ah well," you may be saying, "simple sounds great, but it isn't always easy." Your lovely personality self delights in throwing spanners in the works. Well, simple can be easy and the more inclined you are to let it be easy, to allow it to be easy, guess what? The easier it becomes. Notice I said 'allow' it to be easier. Many people are so conditioned to believing life has to be the way it is that they have to learn how to allow it be different. Start playing the game of letting it be easy.

De-cluttering

I'm sure you've heard of the concept of de-cluttering and getting rid of all that stuff which is past its usefulness date and just blocks the flow of allowing your life to be easier. I suggest you consider and start de-cluttering three aspects of your life: your environment, your thinking and your intentions.

Starting with your environment, just look around you now where you are and notice any clutter and notice how you feel as you see that heap of papers there, still waiting to be sorted out, or those other jobs that are still waiting for your attention. Next, do something about it. Now. Put the book down for a moment, pick one small task and deal with it. Deal with it. As the well-known sports equipment advert says, 'Just do it'.

If you did it, notice how much better you feel now. If you didn't do it, why not? Just notice how you feel. It's all useful information.

Imagine how you will feel if you begin to make a habit of simply de-cluttering a bit at a time, in a way you can easily fit in, once you have made a decision to do it. Or, if you prefer a different approach, you can schedule some time to 'blitz' an area, as long as you are committed to your schedule and actually do it! It doesn't matter how and when you do it, just do it. Stop when you reach what for you is a comfortable and de-cluttered environment.

One person's comfortable space is another person's awful mess and vice versa. Terence recently visited a client with a fabulous multi-million pound house, where no expense had been spared in creating an amazing environment with all top of the range appliances and equipment. He said it looked wonderful at first glance but he didn't find it comfortable. He said it felt sterile and empty, looking like a show home but not feeling like a comfortable home. You will know what the optimum environment is for you and can have fun creating it.

That's your external environment. Now turn to your internal environment and start de-cluttering your thinking. When I asked you to take action a few minutes ago, what did you think about it? If your response was along the lines of 'Good idea' followed by you jumping up and doing it, that's fantastic. Give yourself a gold star.

If you started an internal discussion along the lines of 'Yes, I know it needs doing, but I can't do it now because x', or 'I know it looks untidy, but I like it like that', or 'I'll do it later, when I've got more time', you're probably just kidding yourself.

How good are you at making decisions? Are you a clear thinker, who can quickly evaluate and make decisions? Do you sit on the fence endlessly weighing up the pros and cons of even the tiniest decision you have to make, giving it far more time and attention than it really merits? Or do you sometimes feel so overwhelmed by all that's going on that even the smallest decision is a major event? You probably have a mixture of responses in different situations, but your life can become easier and simpler as you practise de-cluttering your thinking.

Indecision is a major contributor to everyday stress

You have a lot going on, your mind is busy, and you have decisions to make. You want to get it right and you tie yourself up in knots agonising over this. You procrastinate and prevaricate and the decision still needs making, maybe preventing you from giving your attention to other decisions which are now backing up and your stress level is rising....

In the overall scheme of things, the decisions you agonise over are seldom of great importance. If they are, you will know, but often minor matters are allowed to assume disproportionate importance and take up time and thinking space which could be better spent on other matters.

A simple strategy to help you with decision-making is to give an issue what seems appropriate attention, make a decision and then *make that the right decision*. Cluttered thinkers tend to revisit and agonise over decisions they have made: Was that really the best option? Should I have made the other choice? Will I regret this decision? etc., etc. Once you have made the decision, simply stick to it as the right decision for you now.

In the overall scheme of things, there are few decisions which are truly critical or have a major impact on your life and well-being. Most of the stuff that clutters your head is relatively trivial. Be clear that once you have made a decision, it is the right decision for you at this time and act accordingly.

Decide and abide is a great summing up here. You will be amazed at how much space this can free up in your mind. What a relief!

The third area to de-clutter is the area of your intentions. When you know what you want and what your intention is, it's easier to know where to place your attention, which ultimately affects your decision-making at all levels.

Set an intention to keep it simple and notice the changes happening in your life.

CHAPTER FOUR

100% Responsibility

Dr Joe Vitale went from being broke and homeless to becoming a highly respected and high-earning internet marketing and copywriting guru. I first saw him featured in the film *The Secret* about the law of attraction. Having read a couple of his books and liking his work, I have also attended one of his seminars and find him to be a very heartfelt and inspiring man, who lives life to the full as he now shares his spiritual journey.

Dr Ihaleakala Hew Len

A few years ago, Joe wrote about an amazing man, a Hawaiian psychologist who taught a version of an ancient Hawaiian healing practice called Ho'oponopono. His name is Dr Ihaleakala Hew Len and he had helped to heal an entire ward of mentally ill criminals. He had done this without ever seeing them or talking with them.

After reading what Joe had written about Dr Hew Len, when I heard that he was running a seminar in London, I knew I had go. I was intrigued and wanted to meet this man and check him out.

Eating my words

I remember on the drive down saying to Terence, "I am so excited about this and am open to whatever he has to offer today." I soon had to eat my words, literally. When we arrived we were shown to a table with food and drink on and invited to help ourselves. "Oh, they're bacon rolls. I don't eat bacon. What else is there? Oh, pancakes and maple syrup and jam. I don't eat those. Oh, there's only hot chocolate to drink. I don't drink that."

There was nothing there that I thought I could eat or drink. I felt very disappointed. For a while I stood perplexed, wondering what was going on. Then I asked myself if I would like a bacon roll and some hot chocolate. Yeeeeees! "But I don't eat bacon or drink hot chocolate, because they're not good for me."

For a little while I agonised and then, remembering what I had said on the way there about being open to whatever was on offer, I had a bacon roll and some hot chocolate. They were delicious.

What I realised was that I had been running old 'I don't do this' tapes based on decisions I had taken a long time ago and it was time to update them. You know how it is: you make a decision, for good reasons and it is right for you at that time, but circumstances change as time passes. For examples of this, just look at some old photos which show the life you used to lead. I guess you would make some different choices today.

Realising that I had acted on autopilot without actually considering what I wanted, I then read the notices about the healing properties of the foods and drinks that were being offered and decided to enjoy them. This was a great start to the day.

You are 100% responsible for everything in your life

I have always considered myself to be a 'responsible' person, but I was still shocked when Dr Hew Len opened the day and very quickly told us that we are each 100%

responsible for everything that happens in our lives. "Yes, you are 100% responsible for everything in your life. Absolutely everything." Immediately the room erupted into uproar, as very vociferous and indignant people attempted to argue with him, telling him tales of others' outrageous behaviour towards them, or the dreadful circumstances they had experienced.

In our culture you might expect people to argue with him. Most people are conditioned to putting responsibility, or blame as it's usually expressed, outside themselves to some extent and with many people, most of what happens in their lives. It's the fault of the government, the economy, incompetent teachers, greedy banks, illness, parents, crooks, con-artists, nasty people – anyone other than you.

The tabloid headlines scream as they find someone to blame for the latest misdemeanours. The government spends millions on public inquiries to establish who they can blame for the latest scandal and exonerate themselves. On it goes: 'It's not my fault, someone else is to blame,' they insist.

Back at the seminar, some people left. This was too much for them to take on board. Others, having tried arguing, glared with arms folded, but stayed. Most of us were intrigued.

How do you respond when your beliefs are challenged? Would you be willing to consider the possibility that you could be 100% responsible for everything that happens in your life or consider that there might be some benefits in acting as if you were?

Cause and effect

At the simplest level, responsibility is merely the ability to respond. How you respond in a situation depends on how you perceive the situation, whether you are at cause or effect. The continuum of cause and effect is just a natural part of life. One thing occurs and this causes something else to happen and this leads to something else occurring. A chain of events is created and sometimes it is obvious to an observer how this has occurred. Usually, it isn't obvious. There is so much going on in this busy world that often you can't consciously know how something has come about.

When you are at effect in a situation, you believe that things are happening because of what other people or outside forces of some sort have done. This thing has just happened to you. You can feel as if you're just being blown about in the wind and have no control over your situation.

When you are at cause in a situation, however, you believe that you have created it. You have done, said or thought something which has led to this happening now. You may or may not think you know exactly how this has come about, but you accept that you have been involved in some way, at some level, in creating it. You know that there is so much going on in the world which is beyond your conscious awareness that it is possible you have in some way influenced the situation. This feels much more powerful and puts you in a more resourceful state from which to respond in a positive way. However it has come about, you can take responsibility now and respond in a constructive way.

If you're at effect, you are likely to feel powerless, which of course is a good time to ask for help. Being at effect simply means you are out of touch with all the resources you have available to you. They are there, but you've just lost contact with them.

When you are at cause you become more able to view a situation differently and even appreciate the opportunity which this offers you. If you consider that everyone and everything is interconnected, as both the scientists and spiritual teachers tell us, then your rational and logical mind can accept that at some level, or to some extent, you are involved in everything that happens. With this awareness, you can access your resources more easily and consciously and create what you want.

So where are you in your life?

It's important to remember that everyone in your normal everyday world experiences being at effect and at cause and is somewhere on a continuum between the two of them all the time. Any time you think you have a 'problem' you are to some extent at effect. It's only a big deal if you decide to live there!

Just start to notice where in your life you feel at effect and where you know you are at cause and where you are on the continuum between them. It's all useful information. Wherever you are is perfect and that applies to the whole of your life.

Since you're reading this book I am assuming that there are some things in your life that you would like to be different and are open to discovering how things could be for you.

As I ask you to consider your current creation, your current life, notice what comes to mind first. Spiritual teacher Lola Jones describes the mind as 'a wrong-seeking missile', so it is perfectly understandable if you come up with a list of perceived 'problems'. This is an opportunity for some reprogramming and if you've described some happy, enjoyable aspects of your life it's an excuse for some celebrating. In my book, nothing is too insignificant to celebrate. It's the best way to attract more of what you want.

You may not yet wish to take things as far as Dr Hew Len suggests and take 100% responsibility for your life, but maybe you are open to reconsidering and wondering where you might modify some of your responses to current events in your life.

Wherever you are in your life is always a good place to start. Now is where your power is. You can always choose to take more responsibility for what you are creating. Maybe like many people you spend a lot of time banging on about the past or fantasising about the future, and could benefit from spending more time in the present. Probably, almost everybody could benefit from spending more time in the present. This is all you have. This is the moment of choice. This is the moment of power. It's yours for the taking.

You choose your life and the choices you make create your reality

When I was a child it was a rare treat in my family to have ice cream, and vanilla ice cream was the only option. When I was seven I went into hospital to have my tonsils removed. My strongest memory of this experience is the delight of having Neapolitan ice cream, with three flavours – chocolate, strawberry and vanilla. I had never seen this before and was amazed to discover that this was available. Last week on a visit to the cinema, I counted the ice cream options available. There were sixteen to choose from.

One of the paradoxes of modern life is that all around us we are bombarded with choices and yet so often people feel they have no choice in life. It is so easy to lose sight of the choices you have in your life and also so easy, if you want to, to begin to adjust your focus and expand your vision.

As you choose to become more aware of the choices you have available, you can take more responsibility for the choices you make. Right now you are reading this book. You have a choice whether to read it or not. As you read it you have a choice whether to read it with an open mind, a sceptical mind or a whole variety of options. You have a choice whether or not to follow the suggestions offered, as you consider taking more responsibility for your life now.

When I started working as a stress-management consultant, I would always end the first session by recording a twenty-minute relaxation tape for my clients, giving them the instruction to listen to it once a day and come back in seven days. I was amazed by how many people didn't do it. All they had to do was to sit down and listen to it, but they didn't. They paid for my advice, agreed to listen to the tape and then found so many excuses for not doing it.

I know now that if people are ready and willing to make changes, they will and if they aren't yet ready and willing, they will become very creative in maintaining the status quo, in spite of what they say they want.

Having studied many therapies, healing modalities, personal development and spiritual development paths, I have learned that all of them are effective for some people and none of them are effective for all people. Much as many practitioners and followers might like to claim, none of them is the truth, the one way, the solution the world has been waiting for.

Each of them is simply a tool which may help people who are taking responsibility and want to create different experiences in their life. No doubt you have heard the old saying 'When the student is ready, the teacher will appear'. It doesn't matter what the teacher is teaching. The power lies within the 'student' and their willingness to play the game and practise what is on offer. No therapist cures anyone. No healer heals anyone. You cure yourself, heal yourself, create what you want in your life when you take responsibility for your life and are willing to allow change to occur.

Your life is the playing out of the choices you are making

You are always making choices in your life and the vast majority of them are made unconsciously and serve you very well. However, some of them may be based on old stories, which could benefit from a conscious update. Life as you experience it is the playing out of the story you are telling. No doubt you have developed habits concerning your particular story which keep you telling a story that is less pleasing than the one you would like to be experiencing. Everyone does this at some time, to some extent.

The way to change this is to take responsibility for your wonderful, unique story, which you have developed based on your perceptions, experiences and, maybe, mistaken beliefs. You can start telling a better feeling story right now if you want to. Have you noticed how you may have had experiences in your life which at the time seemed awful, but now viewed in a wider context, seem fairly minor? Time and distance help you gain a different, more balanced perspective. When you're in the middle of an intense situation, things do get out of proportion and can seem a lot worse than they are.

Start telling a better story

If you want to be living a better story, you have to start telling a better story. I love the saying 'It's never too late to have a happy childhood'. Many of your beliefs about yourself and the world were formed in the first seven years of your life, based on your subjective experiences in a world you didn't understand. They include things told to you by the adults around you and things which you interpreted for yourself. None of it is absolutely true. It's all a story now.

So what stories do you tell about your childhood? I could tell you about the old dragon of an infant teacher who made a big impression on me when I started school. I was a timid five-year-old who lived on a farm and didn't have much interaction with the wider world. It was a huge shock for me to see this teacher who was in charge now, this very large and seemingly very old woman dressed all in black, who never smiled, hitting children on the head with their hard-backed reading books if they made too many mistakes. I was terrified of her.

In contrast, when I was nine I had a truly wonderful teacher, Mrs Bott. She was very kind, laughed a lot and really knew how to inspire and encourage children to give their best. I really blossomed in her class.

As I think about my infant teacher now, the first image that comes to mind is of her sitting at her table at the front of the class, hitching up her long black skirt to reveal her knee-length bloomers and reaching into a pocket on the leg to retrieve her handkerchief. I remember staring in disbelief at this and not daring to laugh at the time, but I'm laughing now!

I am also aware that my preference for keeping out of harm's way led me to focus and pay great attention to learning to read. I learned quickly and kept my head intact. I also developed a love of reading which gave me access to wonderful worlds beyond my everyday reality. So I am grateful for her part in this, which is still a pleasure in my life.

You create the story of your past right now and if your story is a less than happy one, start looking at it again from your current resourceful adult state and see how many things you can find to appreciate about it. Remember, you get more of what you pay attention to. What you appreciate appreciates.

Similarly, consider your story of your present now. Right now look around you, wherever you are and notice three things to appreciate. Notice those little everyday things that you usually take for granted and take a moment to appreciate them and the positive feelings that noticing them brings to your life now.

Now consider your future. Whatever your stories about the past and the present, remember that now, right now, is the moment of power and you can actually start to create the future of your dreams. We will be looking at this in detail later on, but, for now, you can just ask your unconscious mind to start supporting your conscious mind in opening to the possibility of creating the most amazing future for you.

You can think whatever you choose to

Whatever your past is, whatever your apparent current reality, you can gain a different perspective and create the life your heart or your inner being truly desires. You may be accustomed to thinking that this is all airy-fairy nonsense, in which case please know that uncensored thinking can be very detrimental to your well-being. You can think whatever you choose to. If you want a better life, start thinking better feeling thoughts and become open to the possibility of a happier, more enjoyable and rewarding life. It's yours for the thinking.

Hawaiian healing

As the two days with Dr Hew Len progressed he told us how he had worked with the ward of mentally ill criminals. Their situation was pretty grim by anyone's standards. Many of them were permanently restrained, even shackled to walls because of the level of violent behaviour they expressed. There were lots of disruptions and assaults on the staff and consequently a high turnover and very low staff morale.

Dr Hew Len never met or spoke to any of the inmates. He had access to their files and would study each person's file in turn. He fully believes that he is 100% responsible for everything in his life and that everyone is interconnected, such that what happens in anyone's life is present in everyone's life. As he looked at a file, he would feel the other person's pain and accept it as his pain. Then he would clear that pain in himself using his Ho'oponopono method. He did this process regularly with each file.

Very soon the staff on the ward noticed that things were getting better. People were calming down and behaviour was improving. The whole atmosphere changed. People who had previously had to be restrained were able to be free, violent behaviour and assaults on staff declined and stopped. The whole situation turned around to such an extent that after eighteen months the ward was closed down because it was no longer needed.

Dr Hew Len describes his work as a process of cleaning and erasing, through the repetition of four simple phrases:

- ♥ *I love you.*
- ♥ *I'm sorry.*
- ♥ *Please forgive me.*
- ♥ *Thank you.*

In the seminar Dr Hew Len invited us to bring to mind a situation in which we had felt aggrieved or badly treated. Remembering the other person involved, we then began repeating these four sentences over and over. I love you. I'm sorry. Please forgive me. Thank you.

Return to a state of love

You simply hold a person or situation in mind and repeat these phrases, whatever the story around them. You ignore the story and repeat these phrases. You are dealing with yourself here and these words are just the pointer for you. Ultimately forgiveness is about putting aside any judgements and blame of others involved and allowing yourself to return to a state of love.

I don't yet know many people who can operate with his level of awareness and take 100% responsibility in the way that Dr Hew Len does. However, anyone can aspire to this and start practising. If you get hung up on the words, you can simplify it even further and just repeat 'I love you' to any person, situation, memory, where you experience any discomfort of any sort. If this is challenging for you, please know that it gets easier the more you practise.

You can choose to hold on to being right as you have perceived things, or you can choose to feel better. Dr Hew Len also said that you don't even have to mean it, just be willing to say the words. As you repeat these words your sense of grievance lessens, your feelings begin to soften and you begin to feel better.

As you take more responsibility for your life, you will make better choices, which are more in alignment with your heart's desires. As you make better choices, and are doing what feels right for you, your life gets better. You can create a positive spiral, an upward spiral. We often hear people talking about things descending in a negative spiral, where things get worse and worse. What they don't yet realise is that they can create the opposite: a positive spiral so that their life gets better and better in a continuous upward spiral path.

There is a saying **'Energy flows where attention goes'.** Put your attention on creating an upward spiral and see where it takes you. Wherever you are in life, you can start this now. You are on the path towards taking 100% responsibility for your life now.

The more responsibility you take for your life, the better it gets.

CHAPTER FIVE

All Emotions Are Positive

Life is supposed to feel good

How do you respond to that statement? When I first heard it from Esther Hicks, I had to stop and consider it as I had never heard that before and it sounded a bit radical to me. I know this may sound a bit woo-woo or fluffy, when I tell you that Esther says she channels some other-dimensional beings collectively known as Abraham, who say they are pure source energy. However, the important thing for me is that the information Esther shares is really practical, down-to-earth, useable 'how-to' information for dealing with the nitty-gritty of everyday life. So I'm not bothered where she says it comes from, as I have found it very helpful and so have many people I know.

One thing I really like about Esther is that she presents in a way which is very uplifting and entertaining. She always listens very respectfully and compassionately as people tell their tales of their life experiences and what's happening and what 'problem' they have now. She also uses humour very skilfully as she exaggerates stories of people's behaviour to point out how ridiculous it can often be if they get too hooked up on self-defeating behaviour, trying to be right or make other people wrong.

My favourite fridge magnet says 'Blessed are we who can laugh at ourselves, for we shall never cease to be amused'. That always interrupts any tendency I might have to be taking life a bit too seriously. You might like to try this, too.

I now choose to believe that life is supposed to feel good, because I'm happier thinking that. One of my concerns as I trained to become an interfaith minister was how so many people from different faiths and spiritual traditions took their spirituality so seriously and carried it heavily, more like a burden than a joyful expression of life. Po-faced spirituality doesn't work for me. I've always preferred the image of the laughing Buddha to that of the crucified Christ, much as I appreciate the real teachings of Jesus.

It just doesn't seem right to me now to think that life could be meant to feel other than good. Like everyone else, you have feelings and you are always feeling something. Your different feelings are called emotions and are commonly labelled 'positive' if you like them and 'negative' if you find them uncomfortable or painful, even. To me, they are simply an indication of how in tune you are with your heart's desires or inner guidance or source. How you are feeling is an indication of how much you are letting your genie out and are on track to what you want, or are closing down and veering off-track. The more on track you are, the better you feel and the further off-track you get, the more uncomfortable you feel.

Your emotions let you know where you are

There is a goal or intention or something you want to create or attract into your life and your emotions simply let you know where you are in relation to that. They provide vital information for your guidance. It's all useful information and, in this sense, all emotions are positive. They simply let you know where you are in relation to where you want to be. Remember, there is no such thing as failure, only feedback. What you're feeling is feedback and what you do with it is your responsibility and your choice.

Often people resist the less comfortable emotions. In our stiff upper-lip traditional culture feelings have often got a bad press:

> *'Don't be a cry baby'*
> *'Strong people don't cry'*
> *'Oh, she's so emotional and irrational'*
> *'Keep calm and compose yourself'*
> *'There's no need to get angry'*

Any display of emotion is often seen as a sign of weakness and emotions are to be controlled, so that you can feel more in control of your life.

In my view, being in control is just an illusion, but often a very compelling one. There is so much going on in your life, in your environment, in this country, in this world – most of which you don't know about – so much going on that you can't possibly be in control. It's human nature to want to feel in control. It's a ridiculous notion and life gets a lot easier if you decide to accept that, allow your genie to guide you as best you can and just go along for the ride.

It's a matter of finding the balance which best supports you at present. If you feel you have little or no control you may feel that you are blowing in the wind.

Sometimes that feels good and fun or exciting and sometimes it can feel uncomfortable or alarming. You may feel that you have a lot of control and sometimes that feels good and sometimes it can feel really hard work. What suits you at present?

Returning to emotions, age-old phrases such as 'feeling high as a kite' or 'feeling down in the dumps' are widely used and suggest that some emotions are higher and some are lower than others.

This was recognised long before scientists started telling us that everything in the universe is made up of the same thing and that everyone and everything is vibrating energy. What differentiates things is the frequency at which that energy is vibrating. This so-called physical world is perceived as having solidity. Although they appear to be solid, the chair you're sitting on now and the book you are holding and everything else around you is simply vibrating energy and the lower the vibration, the denser or more solid it feels.

You are vibrating energy and you are vibrating according to your feelings. In the diagram on the next page you can see an arrangement of emotions according to their vibrational frequency in relation to each other.

Emotional Vibration Chart

Bliss	*Expanded, Higher Frequency Vibrations*	
Ecstasy		
Freedom		
Joy		
Love		
Passion		
Enthusiasm		
Happiness		
Optimism		
Hopefulness		
Curiosity		
Acceptance		
Contentment		
Emptiness		
Boredom		
Pessimism		
Frustration		
Irritation		
Overwhelm		
Disappointment		
Doubt		
Worry		
Anger		
Jealousy		
Blame		
Hatred		
Fear		
Grief		
Shame		
Apathy		
Despair	*Contracted, Lower Frequency Vibrations*	

Look at the chart and see how it fits for you. Some of the emotions are very close to each other in vibration and this chart is intended merely as a guide for you. I was first introduced to this concept by Abraham Hicks and this is my version. If your experience is that some are in a slightly different order, that's your reality and how it is for you. Personalise the chart if you wish and add any others that you would like to be included. It's great that you are so aware of your emotions and their frequencies.

When your emotions are at the lower end, in blame or grief for example, your experience and awareness contract. You feel restricted, close down and go into yourself. You have a closed mind, which becomes disconnected from the world around you. Your world can become a very dismal and limited reality.

Conversely, when you are experiencing higher frequency emotions, for example optimism and enthusiasm, your awareness expands. Your mind opens up to more and more possibilities and you feel more connected with the world in which you live. Your world becomes a much lighter and more expansive reality.

When you feel miserable, you don't like the world and when you are happy you love the world and all your amazing companions here. Well, more of them, anyway.

What are you feeling now?

Look at the chart and identify which emotion you are feeling now. Whatever it is, wherever you place yourself on the chart, it is just information. Play with this. If you are lower down the scale, look around you or think about your life and find three little things to appreciate. Keep expressing appreciation until you notice that you have started feeling better.

If you start higher up the scale, do the same thing. Find three things to appreciate and keep appreciating them until you notice that you are feeling even better.

If you think this is silly and don't want to play, just notice how you are feeling and be kind to yourself.

In the flow of the river of life, emotions are constantly changing and moving. When you are aware of your emotions you can guide your life more easily and comfortably. Any emotion is simply information telling you whether or not you are on course in your life.

Think of an aeroplane and its automatic pilot. What a great idea: the plane can fly itself. What many people don't know is that the course is set, but the plane doesn't fly straight to its destination. On average, for 95% of the flight time it's off-course, but it duly arrives at its destination. It's affected by the weather, the environment through which it is flying. It is continually going off-course and is constantly adjusting to get back on course. Consistently. That's just how it operates.

Similarly, in your life when you pay attention to your emotions and notice where you are in relation to where you want to be, you can simply get back on course if you need to. You can develop your own autopilot system through noticing where you are and practising moving up the scale. Just like any other new skill, the more you practise, the easier it gets.

Sometimes you might not want to experience strong, lower vibration emotions. You might be afraid or wish to avoid discomfort. By repressing your emotions, you will create a backlog, which will build up every time you push another uncomfortable feeling down to join it, until one day you are surprised by how strongly you feel and react to a relatively minor situation.

Let it flow and let it go

The skill is to simply feel your emotion as it is, let it flow and let it go. One way to do this is to recognise and name the emotion: "Oh, I'm feeling sad." With the awareness that this is just information, and that the feeling will pass, you can breathe into the sadness and, as you breathe out, let it go. Repeat this a few times until you notice that you are feeling better.

As you learn to flow your emotions you will find that you can become aware of a lower vibration, such as sadness, without affecting your overall sense of well-being. With practice you can just dip into it, acknowledge it and pop out again.

You may be in a situation where you suddenly experience a strong emotion, which may be connected with something currently happening in your life or may come out of the blue. For some reason, your unconscious mind is throwing this up into your awareness now. This may not be convenient if you're in the middle of a meeting or in a situation where it would not be appropriate right now to burst into tears or fly into a rage.

What you can do, rather than just try to stuff it down, is to acknowledge it, thank your unconscious mind and agree to deal with it later at a more convenient time. This may sound a bit fanciful or unrealistic, but, with practice, you can do it. It's a good idea to develop a harmonious working relationship with your unconscious mind, which, after all, only wants to help you.

One of the gifts we each have in this human experience is the wonderful emotional guidance system. This unique system, which you can guide, is your feedback system letting you know where you are on your desired route. It's simply information about your vibrational frequency. You might sometimes think that it is unpleasant or unhelpful, but it is just your unconscious being helpful, from its perspective.

What you do with the information is entirely up to you. The lower frequencies become less pleasant the lower you go and, when you notice this, you can use it as a trigger to get yourself back on course and more in alignment with your inner being, your heart's desires.

Whatever meaning or purpose you give to your life, it's always useful to know how you're doing. The more on track you are, the better you will feel, the happier you are, the more expansive your life becomes and the easier life just flows for you.

Being somewhat slow on the uptake with modern technology, I have only recently started to use a satnav in my car. I preferred to use a map and avoid having an insistent voice constantly interrupting my enjoyment of the music I love to listen to in the car. I now wonder why I never wanted one before, as it makes finding my way to new places so much easier.

Recalculating

I love the way it calmly tells me that it is 'recalculating' if I have misinterpreted the instructions. No panic. No drama. No recriminations. Simply 'recalculating'. I now use the word recalculating as a pattern interrupt when I notice myself visiting a lower vibration frequency. "Recalculating. I can think better than this etc." I instantly start feeling better and it gets easier with practice.

Now you may be thinking: Well that sounds okay for everyday ups and downs, but what about when you feel stuck right down in a very unresourceful-feeling space?

It's just the same – you can practise and learn to start to lift yourself up out of this stuck-feeling place to a slightly better feeling place. Have you ever seen a space ship launch? It doesn't just go 'whoosh' from sitting firmly on its base to hurtling off at great speed. The countdown is completed, you know something is happening because you see some flames and then the rocket seems to hover. It's no longer where it was, it's lifting off before speeding off.

Once you have identified where you are in a 'low' place, by observing and naming the emotion you can start your 'lift off' thinking one better-feeling thought at a time.

I am feeling sad now and this is where I am. Recalculating. I can think better than this. What would feel a little bit better right now? Well, maybe I can just... and you're getting ready to move. It's about gently remembering that you really are a powerful creator and you can focus your thinking to allow yourself to start feeling better now.

Be kind to yourself

Wherever you notice you are on your emotional chart, the most important thing to do before attempting to move is to be kind to yourself. The lower down the scale you go, the more of a challenge this can present, especially if you have developed the habit of berating yourself.

For most of her life my client Sophie had experienced bouts of depression, which were very debilitating. For many years she took anti-depressants and eventually weaned herself off them. Some time later, she noticed the old behaviours returning but didn't want to become dependent on medication again.

One day she was developing an internal argument, both wanting to just curl up in bed and do nothing and also telling herself what she 'should' be doing and how she 'should' get on with certain things. Instead of following her usual pattern and struggling to do what she was telling herself she should do, she decided to go with her feelings and go to bed with a hot water bottle and pamper herself.

Later when she got up she felt much better. So this became her strategy. If she felt herself going down and wanted to go to bed, she did, sometimes staying there for the rest of the day.

One day as she took herself off to bed, after a few moments she had a sudden thought. This could be the last day of my life. Would I really want to spend it in bed? The answer was a resounding NO and she jumped out of bed and did some things she really wanted to do. After that she began developing the habit of treating herself kindly whatever she was feeling.

Play with your emotional scale. As with a piano, all the notes are there to be used. If you try to keep yourself comfortably in a small area, you are restricting your life experience. If you play with your emotional scale and practise consciously experiencing higher or lower frequencies than where you currently are, you will discover how easy it can be to change your vibration, you can lose any fear or reluctance you might have had about going down the chart.

Develop your bounce-back-ability

Remember the steps to creating excellence include flexibility. The more emotional flexibility you can practise, the easier it is to develop your 'bounce-back-ability' – your ability to just bounce back up to a better feeling space.

What is important in living the life you want is how quickly and easily you bounce back if you do go down and off-track. Life is for enjoying and exploring and experimenting. You are creative energy which cannot comfortably be too restrained and restricted. The plan you create for yourself is a fiction and it is inevitable that, at times, with the rest of life intervening as it does, you deviate from what you had in mind.

So what? In this life, nothing is permanent. You have probably heard the phrase 'This too will pass' used by people in a 'difficult' place. Yes it will and you can develop your bounce-back-ability to help it on its way.

When you know that you can always bounce back, you can free yourself of your self-imposed restrictions and really start to enjoy life more and more. You can let go of old habits of playing safe and trying to stay comfortable in the middle and allow yourself to soar in the higher frequencies.

Simply experience more of who
you really are.

CHAPTER SIX

Your Beliefs Create Your Reality

A couple of years ago, Terence and I went on one of our adventures, to the beautiful Hawaiian island of Kauai. We had previously been to Big Island and loved the friendliness and variety of the people we met there. When we heard of a spiritual retreat being offered on Kauai, an island which we had been told was exceptionally beautiful, we went for an adventure, in very high spirits and full of anticipation. We were there to experience the wonderful surroundings and spiritual energy of this fabulous place.

Reality clashes

We really enjoyed exploring the island and one day our group leaders took us to a spectacular beach. As we approached the path leading down to the beach, we saw the big red warning sign 'Danger No Swimming' beneath a picture of a drowning person. It told us of the dangerous currents off the shore, how many people had drowned here in the previous year and that absolutely no swimming was permitted here. Okay with me.

Our intrepid leaders, however, told us that we could, actually, go into the sea, but only for a distance of ten metres. The rest of the group wanted a swim and so they were told to stay within ten metres of the edge of the water. That was okay, but they mustn't go any further out because it really was too dangerous.

Terence and I found a shady tree to lie under and soaked up the beauty of our surroundings: the long stretch of golden sand; the stunningly blue water with the sunlight dancing and sparkling on it; the lush, green 'tropical paradise' vegetation around the bay; the relaxing sound of the water lapping the shore. It was blissful, absolutely blissful. We felt so blessed and at one with the world.

Meanwhile, further along the beach, the rest of the group played in the water and then our group leaders parked themselves on the beach and spent time happily topping up their suntans. Suddenly, horror of horrors, they saw one member of the group being carried past them by the current in the sea.

Imagine their consternation as they leapt to their feet and ran along the beach unable to do anything, while Pete was swirling further away from them in the water. They were panic-stricken and absolutely distraught as Pete was swept along and all they could do was watch helplessly. Eventually, he came to shore, alive and well and unable to understand all the fuss and bother that greeted him.

As a child he had lived on the seashore, learned to swim in the sea and had many years' experience of swimming in the sea. He knew that when he got picked up by the current all he had to do was to relax, because if he struggled he would create difficulties for himself. So, he could relax and enjoy the ride, knowing that eventually he would be deposited on the shore. He had had a great time.

Terence and I were oblivious to all of this going on until it was time to regroup and leave. Our group leaders were still very upset by what had happened, while Pete just shrugged off suggestions of his irresponsibility, recklessness, etc. with the question, "Why bring us to the beach if you don't want us to swim?"

We found this story of the clash of different realities very amusing. Remember Chapter One and the pre-supposition 'reality is a construction'. My reality was that we were having a fabulous time on a glorious beach. The group leaders' reality was that it was only safe to venture so far into the water and Pete's reality was that here was a great playground and he was here for the ride.

The NLP communication model

To get a better understanding of how you create or construct your reality we'll now look at what you do with all the millions of bits of information which are constantly coming your way. Millions of bits every second and only seven, plus or minus two, coming into your conscious awareness at any one time.

My version of the NLP communication model in the following diagram is a simple representation of what goes on.

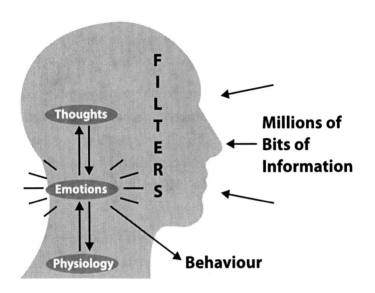

Deletion, distortion and generalisation

Millions of bits of information are constantly streaming into your unconscious awareness. Your unconscious mind sorts these through the three filters of deletion, distortion and generalisation, according to programmes you are running, such as memory, beliefs and values.

Deletion means that a bit of information is simply dismissed. It's not important or relevant at the moment and so is deleted. If you've ever read a document once and then reread it and found that it contained information that you never took in before, that's an example of deletion. The information was there all along, but was filtered out by deletion the first time you read it.

Distortion involves expanding your perception of something to include different, new information and still recognise it. If your colleague turns up wearing glasses when he's never worn any before, you still know it's him. You have distorted what you see to make sense of your experience.

Generalisations are sweeping assumptions you make. You experience things a certain way and expect them to be like that again – for example, you have a lot of issues with a car and make the generalisation that that particular brand of car is unreliable.

Your sixth sense

Every bit of information is taken in through your senses and the traditional NLP model, and many people's thinking, limits you to five senses: seeing, hearing, feeling, smelling and tasting. However, you have sensory experiences beyond these. Sometimes you just know or 'sense' something, don't you, even though you don't know how you know it? You are using other senses which you just haven't been taught how to recognise. As a baby you were taught this is seeing, hearing, feeling, smelling, tasting and those who taught you probably missed out teaching you about any other way of 'knowing'.

If you include a 'sixth sense' to encompass any 'knowing without knowing how you know', you immediately expand your awareness of the possibilities in your life. You can call this your sixth sense, intuition or gut feeling. We all have these experiences and learning to notice and recognise them alongside your other five senses is very useful in helping you in consciously creating your reality.

Thoughts, emotions and physiology

So, information comes in through the senses and then through the filters of deletion, distortion and generalisation to create thoughts. Both your thoughts and your physiology determine your emotions. This emotion determines your behaviour. Your behaviour is always dependent on your emotional state. You also know from the previous chapter that your emotions determine the vibrational frequency you are sending out. The more positive you are feeling, the more positive your behaviour will be and vice versa.

Thoughts and emotional state affect each other and physiology and emotional state also affect each other. There is a constant flow between them all and, of course, a constant flow of new thoughts. Consequently, your thinking and behaviour are constantly adjusting and changing as you receive more and more information.

This is my version of the NLP model, which is just a model, a way of making sense of how we experience our world. Remember, whatever you think you are, you are always much, much more than that. This is the model that works best for me and is pretty simple. As you know by now, simple works best for me. Having some understanding or awareness of how you communicate with yourself is one key to empowering you to make changes in your life.

Your life is all about communication – how you communicate with yourself and how you communicate with those around you and the big, wide world. You can't **not** communicate. You are always sending and receiving messages and information. How often have you heard someone say something along the lines of "She won't communicate with me"? They think that because the person won't talk to them, she isn't communicating with them. In fact, she is communicating very clearly, it's just not in the way the first person would like. Even when you think you are saying nothing, you are always communicating. You can't **not** communicate. Your emotional state is always sending out a vibrational frequency which affects and influences the world around you.

I wonder if you believe that or are willing to believe that. What you believe determines how you perceive yourself and the world, how you make choices in your life, the decisions you make, how limited or expansive your life is.

Beliefs

So what exactly is a belief? It is simply a habitual thought that you hold as being true for you. If you think a thought often enough, it becomes a belief. That is such great information. You can believe whatever you want to. You just have to think it often enough and your helpful unconscious mind will find supporting evidence for you. How empowering is that?

Earlier I spoke about the human fear of not being in control. There is so much beyond you that you can't control, but the good news is that the one thing you can control is your thinking. You may not yet be in the habit of consistently controlling it, but we'll look at that later. For now, hold it as a possibility and a skill to practise.

Your habitual thoughts become your beliefs and your beliefs create your reality. You are probably aware of many of the beliefs you hold and are also probably unaware of some of the beliefs you are running unconsciously. Over the years, you have taken them on from others, especially in childhood. If your parents believed, for example, that the world is a very dangerous place, or people can't be trusted, or you have to work very hard to earn a living, etc., you are likely to have heard this over and over and taken it on as true.

Then, maybe years later, as an adult, you wonder why your life is not going the way you would like it to, you start to examine your beliefs and realise which old tape you have been running, which has been running your life.

You will have taken on beliefs from the media. If you regularly read a particular newspaper you will read the same messages over and over again and take them on. You will have taken beliefs on from your peer group, from teachers, from your life experiences. You will have drawn conclusions based on your perception of your experiences and will have taken them on as beliefs. People formulate mistaken beliefs based on a limited understanding or view of events which have led them to certain conclusions and beliefs.

Have you ever met someone and formed a less than favourable opinion of them based on your interaction with them on that occasion? Then, when you have subsequently got to know them better, you have discovered things about them which completely change your opinion of them? Most people have had this experience at some time and, knowing how much information you must have deleted, distorted or generalised on the first occasion, it's easy to see how this happens.

Often people consider their beliefs to be absolute truths and unchangeable for them. 'This is what I believe. It is true and sacrosanct'. When people tell me this or something similar as justification for holding on to a belief, I'm likely to ask them how helpful or useful this belief actually is in their life now. It may have served them well once, but life is continuously changing and moving on. Maybe it's time to create some new beliefs to support a better present and create a better future.

First you have to be willing and open to this. There is an old saying that 'If a person is unwilling to believe something, no proof is adequate; if a person is willing to believe, no proof is necessary'. If you have ever been caught up in an argument and tried your best to convince a disbeliever of something which you 'knew' to be true, you will know what I mean here.

It's curious how attached people become to their beliefs and lose sight of how temporary some of their beliefs have been in the past. Think for a moment of some things that you used to believe. I'm sure you used to believe you were a child, but I'm assuming you don't believe that now. Maybe you used to believe in Father Christmas or that your parents knew everything, or that the political party you support would transform the country when it came to government. You have held and subsequently discarded many beliefs along the way. Remember, a belief is just an habitual thought and you can think whatever you choose.

Angels

In 2002, Terence and I attended a World Angel Day event in London and met an amazing woman, Doreen Virtue, who trained angel therapy practitioners. We had been given some tickets for this and weren't actually very keen on going, but having been given the tickets we felt some obligation to go. For some time I had been aware of angelic presences when working with some clients and thought I knew all I wanted to know about them.

Little did we know what was in store for us. As soon as we saw Doreen on stage, standing very tall, with her long blonde hair, her long flowing dress and her radiant face, we were mesmerised. We just loved her joyful, open-hearted presentation and her skill in working with people to expand their well-being through their understanding and interaction with angels. By this time, I had obviously come a very long way from my previous "If I can't see it, touch it, prove to my rational, logical mind that it's true, then it isn't." I knew from my experience with clients how helpful it was for some people to believe in angels.

We discovered that Doreen was running a training course in Laguna Beach, California ten days later. We both decided that we wanted to do the training. As I like to help people to help themselves, I was attracted to the idea of teaching people to connect with their angels to get help and guidance, so that they could do it for themselves. Terence liked the idea of just getting his rational mind out of the way, tuning in and channelling information for people. This really was a 'no brainer' for him, which he loves. We both deleted the fact that the course included mediumship training as neither of us was particularly drawn to that.

We were both very keen to attend the training. Terence said he'd ring up the next day and book it for us. "It will be fully booked by now," I said. "We need to go. I'll get us on it," he replied. I wasn't sure about this, but he absolutely believed that we were going. So the next day he rang up and was told that it was full. "Yes, I appreciate that, but I have a big angel standing here, telling me we're going. So can you book us in, please?" After a short pause, he heard, "I think I'm going to get in trouble here, but okay, I'll book you in." His belief that we were going had got us in.

On a gloriously sunny day, ten days later, Terence and I were walking down the main street of Laguna Beach, California which has a fabulous location beside the Pacific Ocean. We were looking around us at all the multi-million dollar beach houses, the abundance of stretch limos and the sparkling ocean.

We were in a bit of a daze. "What are we doing here? We've suddenly had an idea and have flown five and a half thousand miles to California to train as angel therapy practitioners. We've done some fairly surprising things over the years, but have we really lost the plot this time?" As we stood there looking at each other, doing a bit of a reality check, a bus came along the street. As it got close to us, we saw the destination board on the front of the bus change to display the message 'Go Angels'. "Woooo. Did you see that? It said 'Go Angels'. It did say 'Go Angels', didn't it?"

Almost immediately, along came a massive black stretch limo. As it got close to us, the darkened rear window slid down and a cardboard placard was held out about two feet from us, right in our faces: 'Go Angels.'

We just looked at each other and laughed. "Okay," we said, "we're here to play with angels." That was our belief and that was our reality. Later on some people told us that there was a big game for a local Los Angeles sports team that day. That was their reality.

You know that there is always so much more going on than you can be consciously aware of. You are selective about what you pay attention to and what meaning you give to the information. You have formed beliefs in ways that fitted for you at the time you took them on. I wonder how many beliefs you have which are now outdated?

I was quite shocked at the Dr Hew Len seminar to realise that in refusing the food that was on offer, I was just acting from old beliefs that these foods were 'bad' for me. There I was, at a seminar run by a highly esteemed healer and teacher, just dismissing out of hand what he was offering, even though I had said on the way there that I was open to whatever was on offer that day.

So I went back to the table and read all the little notices beside the foods and drinks explaining their healing properties. Then I took them in the spirit in which they were offered. Since then I have been more flexible about what I eat. I still seldom eat meat, but now I consider how it would feel in my body and think fondly of Dr Hew Len when I have the occasional bacon sandwich.

I invite you to start reconsidering some of your beliefs and how well they serve you in living the life you want now.

Geoff was a client who came to me to improve his sports performance and very quickly and easily got the result he wanted. He was absolutely delighted with this as he had been able to impress his fellow club members and win matches for them, regaining his status as a top player.

Some time later, he came back to see me again, this time with a health issue. At that time I had just discovered Ericksonian hypnosis, based on the work of Milton Erickson – a very free-flowing use of language which the conscious mind might not be able to follow easily, but the unconscious mind loves. Geoff relaxed and sat quietly as usual. Afterwards, when I asked the familiar "How was that?" I was somewhat surprised to hear, "When I started listening to that, I thought to myself: What's all this? What a load of old cobblers! Then I thought: No, there must be something really good in this or Shirley wouldn't be telling me it."

He looked at me expectantly. "That's right," I replied confidently. Again Geoff got exactly the result he wanted and was delighted. So, of course, was I and my take on it was that Geoff's belief that coming to see me would help him to deal with his issue was so strong that it did work, even though his conscious mind attempted to undermine things.

Your beliefs are so powerful that it's well worth becoming more aware of them. If your life's not going as you would like it to, there will be some limiting beliefs in operation, otherwise you would be on track. It's as simple as that. You may well be used to thinking that it's due to external events, but now you know differently, or at least you may now choose to start creating new or modified beliefs which will support you in creating the life you want now.

If you think something often enough it becomes a belief and beliefs create your reality. How inspiring and empowering is that thought? As Henry Ford, who founded the Ford motor company, said:

If you think you can or you think you can't,
you're right.

CHAPTER SEVEN

You Can Retrain Your Brain

In 2010, another book came my way which had a very profound effect on me. It was written by an amazing woman who was a neuro-anatomist, a brain scientist. Normally that would have been enough to put me off the book. My filters would have caught that one, but I had heard a bit of the story and was intrigued. Once I started reading, I couldn't put it down.

This brain scientist's work had included discovering and understanding what happens when someone has a stroke. One morning she woke up feeling rather odd and, as her experience progressed, she eventually realised that she was actually having a stroke herself. She found this to be an absolutely fascinating process as she noticed what was happening and, from her experience in her work, was able to understand what was going on in her own brain as it occurred. She observed what was happening as she lost her motion, speech, memory and self-awareness.

It turned out to be a massive stroke in which 90% of the functioning of the left hemisphere of her brain was destroyed. Almost all of her cognitive faculties and rational and logical thought were gone. This left her in a situation where she was almost entirely in her right hemisphere experiences – the creative, intuitive, blissful awareness which usually gets overruled by the left hemisphere brain.

She tells how at first she couldn't understand what people were saying to her from the language they were using, because the words were meaningless to her. However, she could get a sense of what they were saying from their behaviour and manner towards her.

Fortunately for her, her mother totally believed that she could recover from what the experts considered to be a pretty hopeless situation, and cared for her when she was very helpless and unable to function on her own. Her mother then worked with her to help her rebuild her life.

As a brain scientist, she knew how to recreate the neural pathways that structure the brain and was able to recreate major functioning of her brain. She believed in the brain's ability to repair, replace and retrain its circuitry and knew how to treat the brain cells to facilitate their recovery. One thing I found particularly interesting was that she consciously chose to be selective in what she created and some old habits and patterns of thinking, which she no longer considered would be helpful or useful to her, were left out of her new creation.

In effect, she was able to design her own brain, putting in the bits she wanted and leaving out the bits she now preferred to be without. Overall, it took eight years to relearn everyday living and recreate her life as she wanted it. The name of this amazing woman is Jill Bolte Taylor and her book is called *My Stroke of Insight*. It's a fascinating read if you wish to understand more about how your brain works and is a very informative and inspiring story.

Jill now works to educate people about what happens when someone has a stroke and, from her own experience, can explain how they need to be treated and cared for to promote their recovery. She considers that her stroke was a blessing and is very appreciative of her current increased awareness of all that life offers.

Her experiences of being almost totally right hemisphere-aware, where she experienced so much bliss and freedom of awareness, followed by her recreating her brain, leads her to say that you are only ever one thought away from nirvana, from bliss. Another very empowering thought for your consideration.

If you want to live a happy life, think happy thoughts

In my world, life is simple. If you want to live a happy life, think happy thoughts. If you're living a less than happy life, mind your thinking. Your thoughts become beliefs which create your life. So mind your thinking. In this busy, busy life your lovely conscious mind can become a constant chatterbox babbling away, without you paying too much attention to what you are actually thinking.

No doubt you have developed patterns and themes of thinking which you don't question. You would not get much done during the day if you stopped to question every thought. However, once you become aware of an area of your life where you want to make some changes or modifications, then it is very important to become more aware of your thinking in this area.

Start to censor your thoughts and if you're in the habit of believing everything you think, then think again. It's very easy to assume that because you think something, it's true for you. If you **keep** thinking it, then it will **become** true for you. However, many of the thoughts you have may be creating things you don't want in your life now. Start censoring your thinking and upgrading those thoughts which are unhelpful in getting you to where you want to be.

You can think a better feeling thought and start to move up into a more expansive and empowering space **any time you choose.** Now it's very important that when you do notice yourself thinking one of those old limiting thoughts to be very kind to yourself. Jill Bolte Taylor tells how important it was that people should treat her gently and kindly when she was relearning during her process of recovery. If you're learning a new way of thinking, be kind to yourself. Actually, be kind to yourself whatever you are doing!

Many people seem to underestimate the importance of kindness in everyday interactions. We live in a culture which, in its constant striving, often seems to overlook kindness.

Do you drive a JCB, one of those big earth-moving diggers that you can dig a big hole with? Many people undermine themselves and sabotage their goals and aims in life by digging away at themselves with their own JCBs of Judgement, Criticism and Blame. It's so easy to dig yourself into a huge hole which is counter-productive to your well-being. You have no doubt noticed that it doesn't actually help to improve a situation. On the contrary, you feel worse about yourself, your energy contracts and down you go.

Train yourself to treat yourself kindly

Any time you notice yourself judging, criticising or blaming yourself for anything at all, press pause, recalculate and treat yourself kindly instead. Remember that you are always doing the best you can at the time. With the benefit of hindsight, you might think that you were mistaken or unwise to do or say or think what you did, but at the time you were doing the best that you could. So treat yourself kindly as you consider what you might do differently next time.

Treating yourself harshly in any way will only create an internal closing down and disallowing of your well-being. It may be the way you were taught as a child or it may be a behaviour you have learned along the way. That doesn't really matter. What matters now is that you simply set an intention to treat yourself kindly and allow yourself to find ways to do it.

If you start thinking along the lines of 'Constructive criticism can be very helpful,' please reconsider. I believe that criticism is always destructive. Kindness is always uplifting. Which do you want? My favourite quote from the Dalai Lama is "My religion is kindness."

One thing it's important to be aware of is that by following the ideas in this book you will at times find yourself at odds with the way many other people around you think or view the world. Have you noticed how many of them have a rather negative view of life, the 'not too bad' view? In addition to noticing your own thoughts, you may find yourself taking more notice of the language other people around you use. If you've been running with the herd so far and now want your life to be different, you may find that your thinking has less in common with them than it used to. You may find yourself drawn to people with a more positive outlook instead. That's great. They feel better about themselves and enjoy life more.

As you become more of who you truly want to be, your life expands. As you start noticing more positive thoughts, you can amp them up. As you know, you get more of what you pay attention to, so pay extra attention and amp them up. Practise going on a rampage of appreciation. Start appreciating even the tiniest things in your life. Just as you started noticing small things that make you happy, start noticing things to appreciate and then let your appreciation run wild, as one positive and uplifting thought leads to another and another.... It's great fun and you just feel better and better, more and more expansive as your world opens up.

Sometimes you may find your thinking taking you in the opposite direction. Something has occurred and you've jumped on the runaway train of downhill thinking, negative and limiting thinking. There may be things which really bug you and once you start thinking about them, off you go. Remember that it's just a habit you've developed over time and it can be changed once you realise that you want things to be different. Once you are aware that you do this, you can choose some different behaviours to help you to calm down and change your thinking.

Changing your physiology changes your emotion

The communication model we looked at earlier illustrates that physiology influences emotion. So changing your physiology will change your emotion, how you are feeling now.

I invite you to play with this for a few moments:

1. *Sit on your chair and now let your body slump.*
   Let your back bend forward and your shoulders and chin drop. Look down at the floor by your right foot, take a deep breath and tell yourself, "I feel depressed." Really slump down heavily, keep looking down and tell yourself, "I feel depressed." And, temporarily, you do, don't you?

2. *Change state. Jump up and clap your hands together a few times. Then raise your arms above your head like a victorious athlete and tell yourself, "I feel terrific." And you will notice how different you feel now.*

If you want to keep playing:

3. Swap the messages. *As you slump, tell yourself,*
   "I feel terrific." No, you don't. You can't in that position.

4. Jump up, clap your hands, *put them up in the air*
   again and tell yourself, "I feel depressed." No, you don't.
   Your physiology won't let you. So tell yourself how
   good you feel.

You probably didn't realise when you were a child how helpful people were being when they told you to stand up straight or to sit up straight. Be aware of your physiology and play with changing it to change your emotional state. Has anyone ever told you to 'keep your chin up'? There is a lot of wisdom in many of the old sayings.

Smile and save energy

If you want to change your state right now, smile. As you flex your smile muscles this automatically sets off a chemical process in your body, releasing endorphins which help you to relax and release pain, and serotonin, known as 'the happy hormone' which affects your overall sense of well-being and makes you feel better. Did you know that it takes less physical effort to smile than to frown? Smile and save energy!

Have you ever noticed that smiling is infectious? Make a point of smiling more in your everyday life and notice the effect this has on you and those around you.

Another thing you can do to feel better anywhere, anytime, is to pay attention to your breathing. If you're getting upset about something, your breathing will become faster and shallower in your chest. Simply take three s... l... o... w, deep breaths all the way down into your abdomen. As you do this, your mind will start to calm and your thinking will slow down also. Having more space between your thoughts makes it easier for you to reach for a better feeling thought.

You can play with your breathing. Practise some quick shallow breathing and notice how you feel. Compare this with your slow deep breathing. It's all useful information. Develop the habit of noticing your breathing and slowing it when you would like to calm your thinking.

Another easy way to change your state is by listening to music. I'm sure you know this already, but it's good to remind yourself. You can use music to gee you up if you want, or to calm your mind.

If you're feeling a bit more active, yoga is very good for helping you to balance your energy. Meditation also calms your mind and creates space for your thinking. All practical steps you can take to help you retrain your brain.

You saw on the emotional vibrations chart in Chapter Five that when you are feeling the lower emotions, your awareness contracts, your energy shrinks and you feel smaller and less powerful or resourceful. As part of your retraining you can develop the habit of 'stepping back' and seeing the bigger picture in any situation. Ask yourself:

- ♥ *"What else is going on that I may have lost sight of?"*
- ♥ *"What else is possible here?"*
- ♥ *"In the overall scheme of things is this really as terrible/bad/awful as I was thinking?"*
- ♥ *"What is an easy better feeling thought I can reach for now?"*

What if your brain was like a computer and you could programme anything you want into it? Well, maybe it is, and you just aren't aware of some of the programs you have installed. You really can install some new programs, or delete or update old ones. You can delete or update old folders and files or create some new ones that are custom-made for the life you want to be living. Imagine how much fun you can have!

You can create whatever your heart desires

It's your life and you can delete, change, modify or create whatever your heart desires. You can do as much or as little as you want, from a few tweaks to a total makeover. It doesn't matter where you start or why you start. What matters is that you do it in a way that allows you to feel better. Then you know you are on the right track.

So you think of what you want and focus on it consistently and repeatedly. You may have to develop a thicker skin to deal with any naysayers who have a less positive imagination than you, or simply keep it to yourself until people notice changes in you and ask you how you are doing it.

A recent source of inspiration for me has been an elderly lady who lives in the village where I live. Audrey is always smiling and cheerful when I see her. A few months ago she had a fall one day and cut her eye on the road. She already had no sight in her other eye and so to suddenly be bandaged up with no sight at all was a big challenge for her. The prognosis from the doctors was grim. They said it was a very serious injury and thought there was very little chance of her regaining any sight.

Audrey focused on the idea that she would regain her sight and told me very clearly and firmly that she would see again. When people around her were telling her to be 'realistic' and accept her new limitations, she disregarded other people's realities and focused on what she wanted.

She always spoke very appreciatively of the hospital staff and so, of course, they gave her excellent care. She was overjoyed the morning she woke up and was able to distinguish some light, just a tiny glimmer, but she thought it was so wonderful. She certainly knows how to go on a rampage of appreciation and every slight improvement over the following few months was really amped up and celebrated with great excitement and appreciation.

It was so wonderful to hear her greet me with, "How lovely to see you," when I arrived at her garden gate one day and she could see well enough to recognise me from across the garden. She is a wonderful example of the power of positive thinking and focusing on what you want. Bless her.

Affirmations

The way I suggest you start retraining your brain to run the programs you want to install now is by using affirmations. These are statements you make about something you want to believe about your life, and through frequent and consistent repetition they become beliefs which, ultimately, create your reality.

You may have heard discussions about affirmations and their effectiveness. Some people say they don't work. Well, in my experience, they work brilliantly for people who create them carefully and who practise them frequently and consistently, as recommended. You do have to take action and follow through with them.

Have you ever read a book that was filled with exercises, suggestions and useful information, but you told yourself that you'd definitely do them later and then didn't do anything different and so nothing changed? As Pete would say, "What's the point of going to the beach if you're not going to swim?"

I invite you now to think about your life wheel from Chapter Three. Take a look at it, then update it and see how it's looking today. Ask the question:

"On a scale of nought to ten how happy am I?" in each area of your life.

Notice how this may have changed since the last time you did it. It's good to check and keep track of how you are doing. Celebrate any improvements and take as useful any information about changes that you may wish to start making now.

Pick one area of your life where you would like some improvement and follow these guidelines for creating an affirmation to bring this about:

1. *State your affirmation in the present tense: "I am…" as though you are already experiencing what you want.*

2. *State your affirmation positively, saying what you actually want rather than what you don't want. The unconscious mind doesn't recognise negatives such as 'no, not, don't'. How often have you experienced an adult telling a small child, "Don't spill that drink," and how often did they spill it? If I say to you, "Don't think of a potato," your mind will have to go to a potato. It has to think about what you have mentioned before it can think differently. So simply and clearly state what you do want in your life.*

3. Make sure that what you are affirming is believable to you now. However much you think you would like to believe it, you will automatically reject it if it is too far removed from your current situation. If you are focusing on your finances, for example, and you attempt to affirm, "My life is filled with abundance and money flows to me easily," when you are unemployed and broke, you're likely to also think 'No it isn't and no it doesn't,' which will override your positive statement.

4. If you are wanting a big change, that's great. You just have to make your affirmation believable to you now. One way to create a successful affirmation which contains a big want is to start with "I am becoming…" or "I am in the process of…" or "I am happy…" – for example, "I am happy as my body is in the process of becoming slimmer and healthier." I also like to end an affirmation with "and I am living an amazing life."

5. As you state your affirmation, use all your senses to create a full experience of what you are affirming. Notice what you see as you imagine your desired reality, what sounds you hear around you, how it feels, etc. when you have this desired outcome. Notice all the good-feeling thinking your affirmation creates for you and amp it up. Use all your senses and the more feeling you put into it, the more powerful your message becomes and the more quickly you create it in your life.

6. *What else can you come up with to make your affirmations really believable for you, to make them clear statements of what you really want to create in your life and to make them fun? You learn best when you are enjoying yourself, so make it fun.*

Once you have created affirmations, remember them and say them aloud as often as you can. They become installed through repetition. Buy yourself a lot of sticky notes and put them everywhere you can – mirrors, fridge, doors, computer, dashboard. Put them anywhere you will see them often. Repeat them every night before you go to sleep and every morning before you get up. You want your brain to get the message as often as possible.

Becoming a winner

You are constantly training your brain, whether or not you are consciously aware of it. Anna recently took up running and joined a local club. After a few months, encouraged by her co-runners, she decided to enter a race, just for the experience. She enjoyed the event and ran much faster than she had expected. To her great surprise, she came first in her age group, beating over fifty other runners. You can imagine her delight.

That evening she noticed a card on a chest of drawers at home. It was the card her son had made for her birthday seven months previously. She was so used to it being there, she didn't usually consciously notice it. That night she did notice it again and was very surprised to see that it was a picture of her running a race and being first through the finish line. Without realising it, she had been training her brain. When she had received the card, she really loved the picture and seeing herself winning a race. She then forgot about it. Subsequently, she had repeatedly seen that picture and her brain had taken it on and created the experience without her conscious attention to it.

Turning lemon juice into tea

About fifteen years ago I became aware that I was drinking huge quantities of tea, about twelve or fifteen mugs a day, which I decided was possibly detrimental to my general well-being. It also stained my teeth a lot. Reading that hot water with a squeeze of lemon juice would be more healthful for my body, I decided to start drinking lemon water instead of tea.

So one morning Terence brought me an early morning mug of tea and with it, a mug of lemon water and I decided to experiment with an NLP process. I sipped the tea. Oh, it was lovely. As I sipped it I really enjoyed the taste and noticed what I thought and how my body felt. Then I sipped the lemon water. It was disgusting! I shuddered as I tasted it. Yuk. I noticed all of my experience of drinking it.

Then I took another sip of tea followed by a sip of lemon water. As I did so, I started swapping my responses from one to the other. I transferred my earlier thoughts and reactions to the tea to the lemon water and I transferred my earlier thoughts and feelings about the lemon water to the tea.

I was delighted to discover that it only took about six or seven sips for me to change my experiences to the opposite of how they had been previously. I began to really enjoy the lemon water and reject the tea. I was amazed at how easy it was. Ever since then I have intensely disliked tea and absolutely love hot water with lemon, or on its own is just as good. Every so often, out of curiosity, I just check some tea to see how it is now, but it's always horrible and I'm happy for it to stay that way.

Maybe you're getting the idea now that you really can retrain your brain if you want to and it could even be a lot easier and a lot more fun than you might have imagined. As Carl Jung said:

I am who I choose to become.

CHAPTER EIGHT

Four States Of Awareness

In this wonderful, magical world, life is dynamic and constantly changing. Nothing is permanent for you, much as you might like it to be. Your mind, amazing though it is, can only hold a very limited amount of information/knowledge in its conscious awareness at one time. It's part of being human to want to understand and give meaning to life. 'Who am I? Why am I here? What is the meaning of life?'

After spending a great deal of time and energy, over many years, considering such questions, I eventually came to the conclusion that it really doesn't matter what answer you come up with. What matters more is what that answer means to you and how it guides and directs your life, whatever your beliefs. If you are living a life which is happy, joyful, fulfilling and meaningful to you, you've cracked it! Congratulations. Enjoy it. There is more to come.

If you know in your heart, your inner being, that there is more that you want to have, do, or become, congratulations, you're being human. You are part of the creative energy of the universe and that is constantly expanding. You are 'programmed' to have desires and wants. That's part of living. When you stop having desires and wants, you are in the process of dying and I am assuming here that this is not what you are wanting just yet.

Esther Hicks says, "You can't get it wrong and you never get it done." So relax and enjoy the process of living and following your heart's desires.

Beyond words experiences

You know, don't you, that there is far more to this wonderful world than your mind can understand? You also have sublime moments – maybe frequently, maybe only very occasionally – when you just 'know' things that you simply don't have the language to put into words, or think thoughts which explain or express your experience, your awareness. These are 'beyond words' experiences when you are actually accessing and allowing a level of awareness which is way, way more than little you.

We are in this apparently three-dimensional world and we all sometimes have experiences which go beyond this reality into other levels of awareness. Whether you say, as many people do, that you are a human being having a spiritual experience, or whether you say, as Carl Jung did, that you are a spiritual being currently having a human experience, or whether you say, as Michael Bernard Beckwith does, that you are a multi-dimensional being currently living in a three-dimensional reality, doesn't matter. They are all ways of attempting to give meaning to life.

Humans want to give meaning to life as part of their wish to control life. The possibility of being out of control absolutely terrifies many humans and they will go to extraordinary lengths to create amazing theories about how the world works. They may use their intellect to create marvellous fictions and put huge amounts of energy into convincing others of their truth.

One of the purposes of this book is to encourage you to trust and fully enjoy your own reality, your own awareness. However educated, experienced or highly regarded a person may be, if what they say doesn't resonate with you, I suggest you simply respect it as their model of the world, their reality, and choose differently for yourself.

You're right

I was very shocked on the counselling course which started my journey of self-development to learn that other people's opinions were just as valid as mine. On my first NLP training we did an exercise where one person would talk passionately for several minutes about something which they believed strongly. During this time, their partner had to listen carefully and all they were allowed to say was, "You're right. You're right. You're absolutely right." That was a huge challenge for me and certainly helped me to start 'accepting' other people's realities.

Ultimately, you choose what fits for you and it's important to learn to trust your vibes and how things feel for you. You are unique and, however intelligent, educated, tuned in, sensitive or psychic they are, no one else can really know for sure how life is for you. Only you can know that.

Just as the emotional chart shows the expansion and contraction in your sense of well-being, you can also identify four states of awareness which you can experience in your everyday living. The state you are experiencing indicates your current relationship with your inner genie, the powerful being that you truly are.

I first heard these four areas identified and described as levels of consciousness by Michael Bernard Beckwith, spiritual teacher and founder of the Agape International Spiritual Center in Los Angeles. When Terence and I visited Agape and met Michael and his wife Rickie, we received a wonderfully warm welcome as we joined a group of about six hundred people gathered to enjoy an amazingly uplifting, joyful and inspiring experience at one of Agape's regular services.

The first of the four important states of awareness is the victim state, where you feel powerless or have very limited power and are closed off from the positive aspects of your life. Next is the manifester state, where you are flexing your creator muscles and are being proactive in creating the life you want. Then comes a surrender state, where you are more aware of the bigger picture in life and finally, comes the being state where you are totally in harmony, being all that you can be in this world.

Although this may seem like a linear progression, it may be, but it's not necessarily so. It may also be different in different areas of your life, so you may be in one state with one area of your life and in a different state in another area. Suzanne was a very successful executive in her marketing career, with a highly responsible position and clearly a manifester there. Her marriage was completely different, with her repeatedly going into a victim role where she felt unable to make the simplest decisions or feel any power.

It's helpful to understand that this is a very fluid concept and life is continuously changing, so you are never fixed in a state. It's all useful information to help you get an understanding of where you are. Once Suzanne realised what she was doing, she was able to start making changes so that the relationship became more balanced.

Victim state

In the victim state you feel as though you are the victim of life. Someone or something outside of you is doing something to you. You don't like it and you feel powerless to do anything about it. You are putting responsibility for your unhappiness or lack of well-being outside of yourself. Any time you notice yourself thinking along the lines of:

- ☹ *It's not fair*
- ☹ *Why can't I…?*
- ☹ *Why does this always happen to me?*
- ☹ *I'm so unlucky*
- ☹ *They shouldn't treat me like this*
- ☹ *I've been wronged.*
- ☹ *They've ruined my life*
- ☹ *It's the government's fault that I can't…*
- ☹ *The world's against me*
- ☹ *There's no alternative*

then you're in victim mode. It sometimes seems that most members of our society spend most of their time in a victim state, which actually often suits those people in positions of power.

Some people live all of their life in victim state, some people just drop in occasionally. I doubt there is anyone who has never had the experience to some extent. It's just part of being human.

It could be due to mistaken beliefs you have taken on and, as you know, mistaken beliefs are simply the result of insufficient information and you can always learn more. Remember, no matter what you think you are, you are always much, much more than this.

The most pervasive proponents of victim mentality in our current society are the media. The headlines scream the awfulness of life. Disasters, tragedies and woeful tales feed a voracious appetite for bad news. For many people it becomes addictive. If you find that you get fed up with this diet of doom and gloom, there is a simple solution: stop reading the papers and stop watching or listening to the news. However, an amazing number of people are unwilling to do this, in spite of their professed distaste for it.

My mother-in-law, bless her, could not understand why Terence and I didn't regularly read a paper or watch television. "But you won't know what's going on," she would say. "No, we don't want to," we would reply. "But you need to." "We think differently."

She just couldn't understand this and would save the direst articles from her redtop rag. "Look at this." "No thank you." "Look what they're doing now. It's terrible." "No thank you."

You may find yourself at odds with others if you just disengage with these doom-mongers, but I guarantee you will feel much better if you become more selective about what you serve up to your unconscious mind.

Maybe your family or your peer group have taught you to develop victim consciousness with ideas such as:

- ☹ *Good things don't happen to people like us*
- ☹ *It's all right for them, but we can't*
- ☹ *I just can't win*
- ☹ *The odds are always stacked against me*
- ☹ *It's no use even trying*

Wherever it comes from, you take it on as true for you and you feel powerless. To move you along from here, the first thing to do is to recognise where you are. Once you feel and acknowledge this, you can then remind yourself who you really are, remember your powerful genie self and start to retrain your brain. You can start to ask more empowering questions:

♥ *What might I be able to do here?*

♥ *What else can I do here to make this better for me?*

♥ *What do I know that can make a difference for me here?*

♥ *How can I see the bigger picture here?*

♥ *Who do I know who could help me here?*

You can start to make different conscious choices and take different action and this will, of course, change your reality.

Ask for help

Things may have occurred in your life which you didn't consciously choose, which you think you wouldn't want, and which may even be horrendously awful. Once you start taking more responsibility for your life now, however awful your circumstances may have been or may appear to you now, it is possible to start making changes, even if they are only tiny ones to start with. Remember the saying 'A journey of a thousand miles begins with one step' and there are always people around who could help you if you want some help, but you may have to ask. How good are you at asking for help? It usually makes life a whole lot easier to deal with.

Sometimes a person gets to a stage of being so fed up with being a victim that they start getting so angry that they are able to take action and start lifting themselves up and improving their lives. This is an example of the positive power of anger. It can get you moving up the emotional chart. At some point, you say 'Enough' and resolve to make changes. Remember the saying 'Once you make a decision, the universe conspires to make it happen'. Having made the decision you start noticing supporting evidence to make it the right decision.

Manifester state

'The universe conspires to support me' is a very helpful belief to have as part of being in the next state, the manifester. In this state you are developing your power to create and attract the wonderful array of things you want in your life. You may be consciously working with the law of attraction, which simply says that everything is vibrating energy which attracts and is attracted to matching vibration. So if there is something you want, you have to find the appropriate vibration in yourself and allow it to increase, amp it up, and then what you want has to come to you.

You are exercising your creative power and feeling far more powerful than in the victim state. You are taking responsibility for your life and consciously taking action to get what you want in life. You think along the lines of:

- ♥ *I can do it*
- ♥ *If it's possible in the world, it's possible for me*
- ♥ *I am a powerful creator*
- ♥ *I know how to get what I want in life*
- ♥ *I am enjoying the life I am creating*

You feel as though you are more in control of your life. You are creating your destiny. You may consider yourself to be 'lucky', but also know that what you achieve is a result of your choices and the decisions you have made. People who consider themselves 'lucky' or 'fortunate' just keep on finding evidence to support this idea.

When I decided to start calling myself The Happiness Granny it had a big effect on me. Every time I remember that this is what I now call myself, I automatically smile. I am manifesting The Happiness Granny.

As a manifester, you have clear intentions which you consistently focus on. Maybe you are one of those people that others think of as leading a charmed life.

Maybe you think you lead a charmed life. Maybe your whole life or at least some aspects of it just seem to fall into place without any effort on your part. When this happens you are vibrationally lined up with your goal or desires and you manifest them easily and naturally.

Surrender state

Often when people have been highly successful in this material world they get to the stage where they change their focus from themselves and what they can do or get for themselves, and turn their attention outwards to the rest of the world. They move into the surrender state as they become aware that there is a far greater power than their little self operating and are willing to become an instrument or channel for this creative power. They may turn their attention to discovering what they can do for the greater good, for the benefit of their fellow humans.

In this state, people are allowing a greater awareness of a bigger picture in life and the part they can play in it. Often people who have made great financial fortunes become philanthropists and spend their money or use their talents for the benefit of others. Pop stars give concerts for charities. They look around and ask, "How can I be of service here? How can I help other people?"

Also in this channel state are people such as musicians or athletes who have developed a talent or skill to a very high level. When they give an absolutely outstanding performance they often say things like:

- ♥ *"I was really in the zone."*
- ♥ *"It was as if something took over and I wasn't in control."*

Soon after I had trained as an angel therapy practitioner, I naturally wanted to tell people about angels and how they could connect with them for help. So I booked a venue and arranged a talk one evening to introduce people to angels.

About thirty people turned up and we got started. About four or five minutes into my carefully rehearsed talk, I suddenly lost my words. I noticed that the loop of words which was supposed to pass through my mouth was circling around my left knee. I closed my eyes and heard myself say, "I'm being told to shut up here."

So I sat there in front of a group of thirty strangers, with my eyes shut, saying nothing and feeling that I had no control over what was happening. I was not consciously directing this. My anxious little conscious mind did attempt a feeble 'What will they be thinking?'

but I couldn't really connect with it and it floated away while I enjoyed what I was feeling. I felt very expansive, very peaceful, in a timeless, boundless space of immense well-being.

Just as suddenly as it had started, it stopped. The words popped back up into my mind and I gently resumed my talk. I had no idea how long I had been 'out', but when I asked Terence afterwards, he guessed it was about three minutes. It could have been thirty-three for all I knew.

I calmly carried on talking as though this was an everyday occurrence and was intrigued when, during the question time at the end, a member of the audience told me what she had seen. She said that when I started talking, a golden light began to shine about three feet above my head. This golden glow got stronger and, just before I stopped talking, it came down through my crown chakra at the top of my head and, as I closed my eyes, it started flowing down through my head and shoulders and out through my heart to the audience.

Several people smiled and nodded. Others said how beautiful and loving it felt. I just nodded and smiled as though this happened all the time, feeling greatly relieved to hear what they had experienced.

In this allowing state you are able to surrender your sense of control, your desire for control, so that higher vibration energy may flow through you and enable you to achieve previously impossible performances. The divine, more expansive, higher frequency energies are flowing through you and you are happy to allow this.

Being state

The fourth state of awareness is the being state, when source energy, life force, doesn't just flow through you as a channel as it does in the surrender state. Instead, it becomes you and you become it as one. In this state, you are being yourself as a human being and, at the same time, consciously fully allowing the creative energy of the universe to flow through you and as you.

You are living as the fullest expression of the creative you. Maybe you just get a brief occasional glimpse of it or maybe it becomes a regular and fabulous experience. This is who you are here to be and you are expressing it in your own unique and perfect way.

In this state, you are fully living as a human being and as a divine being. You are allowing the grace, the joy, the pure life force energy to flow through and as you. In this state, you are consciously aware of your higher levels of spiritual awareness, although you may not have language to describe or explain these beyond words experiences. It is also a visceral experience – you are aware of your body and feel the source energy flowing through you, with your body also feeling very grounded. You feel fully alive – fantastically, vibrantly, joyfully alive. Your human self and your divine self are consciously co-creating your experience.

In this state, you know your interconnection with all, you absolutely know the oneness of all. You also know that you are inseparable from this. You are this, even though you may be unaware of it for most of the time. In spite of the fact that your limited awareness does not at times include this knowing, it is still so. No matter what you think you are, you are always much, much more than this.

Take a few moments now to consider your life. How often do you have, or have you ever had, the experience of totally and undeniably knowing your being state? If you believe you have never had an experience like this, let your imagination run loose now and get a sense of how this could be for you. If you have had such experiences before, take a few moments to remember them now and how they are for you. Maybe you have had experiences of feeling and knowing that you are one with all when you are out in a beautiful place in the countryside, or listening to some sublime music, or seeing the deep beauty in a person's face, you just inexplicably know.

In her book, Jill Bolte Taylor tells of when she was losing her conscious faculties, her left hemisphere dominated awareness, and she saw her extended arm as blending into the surrounding space. She knew it was her arm, but she couldn't differentiate between her arm and the surrounding space. They appeared to merge and there was no separation between them, as she could see everything as flowing energy.

A couple of years after I was ordained as an interfaith minister, I was pondering one evening the fact that I had done little to promote myself as a minister and was asking myself that wonderful question, "What do I really want?"

As I pondered this, the telephone rang. It was a fellow interfaith minister who opened the conversation with, "Do you want to do a wedding?" He explained that he had had an enquiry from a couple who lived near me, but he wasn't available on the date they wanted. Don't you just love synchronicities like this?

So three months later I found myself having one of the most beautiful and amazing experiences of my life so far, as I conducted a wedding blessing for a delightful couple.

The whole process of creating their ceremony had been an absolute joy. Try as my little mind might, I just couldn't get nervous about it. I knew it was going to be a wonderful day.

As I stood at the front of the beautifully decorated marquee, before the two hundred guests, I felt truly blessed and very alive but with an unfamiliar calmness. I felt very expanded and very present in the moment. I absolutely knew, beyond any possible doubt, that I truly was the presence of love and was powerful beyond words. At the same time, I was very aware and in control of my body and knew that I was there in human form to bless this beautiful couple and their future life together.

This was the highest possible service I believed I could offer and was also the most beautiful and joyful experience I could imagine. As the bride and groom entered the marquee, I could feel the loving energy pouring through my heart and enveloping them. I felt very moved as they walked down the aisle. They both radiated such happiness and I could so easily see their true beauty.

That was the most profound and moving example I can recall of my being state. I feel so blessed every time I think of that day.

Victim, manifester, surrender and being consciousness, are four definable and identifiable states of awareness that you may experience. They could be broken down into subsections, but these are main areas. They are flexible and changeable and you probably visit them all at some time.

Remember, you are human and unless you live a very sheltered life away from mainstream society, you probably have many unexpected and surprising experiences in life. It's all part of the game, part of the fun of being alive at this fast-changing time. You could at any time find yourself in any of these states, or you may at any time choose to move into any of these states.

I invite you to use your immense innate power, your inner genie, to allow any changes or developments you would like to experience and to amp up and really milk all the aspects of your current state that you really appreciate.

CHAPTER NINE

What Do You Want?

Way back, when I trained as a stress management consultant and hypnotherapist, I was so excited and passionate about all the possibilities for assisting people in creating the life they wanted. It was a big adventure and although rather daunting in some ways, it just felt a good thing to be doing. Along with my certificates on the wall I had a simple notice which said 'My reason for doing business is to add value to people's lives'. Twenty-something years later, although many things in my life have changed, that simple statement is still true.

This book has been written with that in mind. I am passionate about sharing what I have learned so that it may add value to people's lives. That's what I want to do. I also want to live with an open heart and an open mind harmoniously creating whatever my heart truly desires. I also want to continue enjoying abundant love, happiness, joy, prosperity, fun, adventure, new experiences….

I'm using the word 'want' in a positive way. Rather than an indication of lack in your life, as it can be used, here it's simply an expression of desire, of moving towards something positive you would like in your life. Express what you want with a lightness of touch and a sense of expectancy.

In my naivety, I was very surprised, when clients started arriving at my door, to discover that everyone who came to see me was more focused on what they didn't want than on what they did want:

> *"I don't want to be depressed."*
>
> **"What do you want?"**
> *"I don't want to feel so miserable."*
>
> **"What do you want?"**
> *"I don't want to feel that life is so meaningless."*
>
> **"What do you want?"**
> *"I don't really know, but I don't want that."*

Some clients were very attached to what they didn't want and could describe at great length why they didn't want whatever it was they had come for help with. Often they had no clear awareness of what they did want instead.

'Away from' and 'towards'

When I discovered NLP, I learned about people's 'away from' and 'towards' strategies and their relative outcomes. How often have you heard of someone who came from a very impoverished background, for example, who decided that they were going to do whatever it took to become wealthy? They had had enough of poverty and the misery it created for them.

So they do well and create their wealth and then things go wrong, their business fails or they lose their job and suddenly they're broke again. They're back in the misery of what they don't want. Often they get themselves together and become successful again, only to repeat the scenario.

What is happening here is that they are running an 'away from' strategy. They are doing all they can to get away from poverty and once they are financially comfortable, the motivation is gone because they have nothing to move away from now. So they stop what they were doing to keep them moving away and, consequently, they lose their money again.

In contrast, someone with a 'towards' strategy is moving towards something they do want. They are being drawn towards something which inspires or uplifts them. So when they achieve one inspiring goal, they keep moving forward as they are drawn to another one. As they move towards what they want, other possibilities begin to open up for them and take them beyond their original goal. They create further desires which keep them moving forward.

An 'away from' strategy moves you away from pain and is fear-based. "I'm afraid I might experience that again and so I must make sure that I don't." A 'towards' strategy moves you towards what you do want because this is a better feeling place for you and inspiration will keep you moving forward.

Right now, what do you want? If you're like most people who perceive a problem or problems in their life, your wrong-seeking missile of a mind will most likely throw up a 'don't want'. That's okay. Your helpful unconscious mind simply wants to keep you safe by drawing your attention to threats.

It's just information and it's what you do with this information that is important here. If you get stuck there and 'awful-ise' your situation, continually beating the drum of what's wrong in your life, you will create more of that. 'Energy flows where attention goes' is another way of putting this.

The wise response is to use this as the 'contrast' which is helping you to identify what it is that you do want. Sometimes people get so bogged down in their problems that they develop tunnel vision and lose sight of the bigger picture. They simply cannot see beyond their current concerns.

Remember that this is useful feedback; whatever you think you are, you are much, much more than that and you have all the resources you need to get you on track. So notice the contrast and get out of there as quickly as you can. Use it as a springboard to a better feeling place. This experience is letting you know your vibration and you can start to raise this, one better feeling thought at a time.

Of all the resources you have available to you in deciding what you want in your life, do you know what is the most powerful? You may think it's your knowledge, your experience, the people you know etc. and these are all important, of course. However, as Albert Einstein said:

"Imagination is more important than knowledge, for knowledge is limited to what we now know and understand, while imagination embraces the entire world and all there ever will be to know and understand."

Read that again. Can you feel that thought opening up your awareness? Doesn't that automatically encourage you to appreciate your imagination?

If you can imagine it, you can create it

So if you're not yet in the habit of letting your imagination run free in matters of what you want, start now. It's curious how many people's minds, when given a piece of unwelcome information, can then take off and add to it many other undesirable possibilities. They probably think they're being prepared for possible outcomes by worrying about them, without realising that, by doing this, they are in fact creating them.

The best definition of worry I've heard is that it is planning a future you don't want. If you keep thinking of some unwanted possibility which might happen, you are lining yourself up to receive it. The vibration you are creating will attract more of the same. Think how much better your life could become if you regularly used your imagination to plan a future based around what you really do want.

You've no doubt heard other people tell you that you could have, be or do whatever you want to, so what stops you? There are three strong fear-based contenders here and maybe you know of more that apply to you. The three I've encountered most often with clients are mistaken beliefs, a limited sense of self-worth and an underdeveloped or misguided imagination.

As you've no doubt noticed by now, mistaken beliefs pop up everywhere. If there's something you've thought of that you want, but you don't yet believe you can have, there's a mistaken belief getting in the way. If you ever hear yourself thinking 'I can't have that, do that, be that,' ask yourself, "Why not?" and up will pop the mistaken beliefs:

> *'People like me don't do that'*
>
> *'I'm not clever enough'*
>
> *'It's too difficult for me'*

Now is the time to ask empowering questions such as:

"Who says so?"

"Do they know everything?"

"Is this really true?"

"How can I help myself with this?"

"Who else could help me with this?"

You will probably find you are running old tapes here and need to remind yourself of the resources available to you.

Lack of self-worth or self-esteem is another big blocker. 'I don't deserve…' 'I couldn't possibly….' Again, who says so and is this really true?

An underdeveloped or misguided imagination is simply due to lack of practice and probably another limiting belief or two. Maybe you've decided that you're not creative.

"I'm just not creative."
Yes you are and you are creating this.

"I don't think that way."
Yes you can.

Remember when you were a child. I'm sure you had a great imagination then. You may even have been told by others to curb it and be 'realistic'. In other words, to buy into their reality. Maybe now, like many people, you find it much easier to imagine an unwanted scenario than a desired one.

Start playing 'what if…?'

Everybody can have a great imagination if they want to. Watch some children's films or fantasy adventure films. Get creative. Just let your imagination run free. Remember, you can do what you like in the privacy of your own head. Play and have fun. This is all part of you allowing yourself to move beyond the self-imposed limitations and restrictions in your life, by a change of attitude and thinking.

What if it were all possible for you, in spite of what you have been used to thinking or what the rest of your world tells you? Just imagine… What if I could…? What might I enjoy? How much fun could I have? Where could I go? What could I really do?

Before we go into details about what you want in different areas of your life, I have one question for you to ask yourself:

If I really could have, do or be anything I wanted, what would it be?

The answer may be something you are already well aware of, or it may come as a surprise. Let's put it another way. The question is:

If you knew that you absolutely could not fail, what would you do in your life?

Ask yourself this question and see what comes up now. This highlights another reason that people don't go for what they want: fear of failure and looking foolish for even thinking it might be possible. Or maybe it's fear of success because you don't know how it might be if you moved out of your comfort zone.

Is it time yet for you to think big? I mean really, really big. Maybe you genuinely don't want anything big or maybe you've been too afraid to go for it up until now. Do you really want to keep playing small or are you going to take this opportunity to start living as a fuller version of the person you can be? Maybe you wonder how much more there could be to life than you have been living and are gearing up now to finding out what actually is possible for you in this wonderful adventure of living on earth.

In our present health-and-safety-gone-mad culture, people are becoming more and more risk-averse. Have you grown accustomed to taking the safe, familiar option rather than the fun, adventurous, awareness-expanding option?

In these uncertain times it is becoming more and more obvious to people that many of the old systems and structures in our lives are breaking down. There is no such thing as a job for life any more, divorce rates are phenomenally high, many people are exploring alternative and non-traditional lifestyles. Technology and life are speeding up so fast and you either jump into the new paradigm or you get left behind.

Now is a new beginning

One day, a few years into my therapy and healing practice, a client, Dave, came to see me. I was very pleasantly surprised when he sat down and took out his shopping list of all the things he wanted. No client had ever done this before. There were about half a dozen items on his list, all positively stated and he told me why he wanted them all in his life now. I listened carefully and was impressed by the thought he had put into changes he wanted to make in his life.

I confirmed that we could address all of those things and then asked him about his leg as I couldn't help noticing how he was limping as he came in.

He had damaged his knee playing hockey the previous day. I asked him if he would like some Reiki healing for it as it was very painful and swollen. He'd never heard of Reiki before, but was willing to find out how it could help him. Half an hour later his leg was pain-free and the swelling greatly reduced.

He was so impressed that he decided to move on from his previously important list and asked me to teach him Reiki instead. I was amused that the one time someone came to me thinking he was absolutely clear about what he wanted, he then saw there was something available to him which he hadn't anticipated and he chose that. He did get the changes he wanted in his life and a lot more as well. His life changed dramatically. He loved Reiki and became a very effective healer.

I loved the way he had decided to make some changes in his life and then recognised and was willing to go with something unexpected and previously unknown, when he became aware that it was available to him. However clear you think you are about what you want, you can never know for certain exactly which way your life will go, once you become more open to possibilities and new directions. That's part of the fun of living.

One of my favourite sources of inspiration, the Persian poet Rumi, wrote:

'Yesterday I was clever, so I wanted to change the world. Today I am wise, so I am changing myself.'

Take a step now towards what you do want as you start to identify this. Let's put your wrong-seeking missile of a mind to good use here and start by taking a quick look at the things you know that you don't want.

On a sheet of paper make a list of the things you can think of which you don't want. Any things you're fed up with, have had enough of, want to end.

Next, take another sheet of paper and make a new, inspiring list. For every item on your first list ask yourself:

"So what do I want instead, now?"

Write this down, making sure it is what you **do** want and is positively phrased. Next, destroy your first list – tear it up and flush it away or burn it. That's gone.

Now return to your Do Want list. Are you aware that there are areas of your life where you feel you are achieving, or being, less than you could or would like to? In the kindest and gentlest thinking you can offer, start to let your imagination run wild. I suggest you be as unrealistic and outrageous as you can currently allow yourself to be.

Start thinking of things that would be fun, joyful, ex-hilarating, hilarious, silly, entertaining, awe-inspiring, uplifting – anything which will allow the free spirit in you to come out and play… and take you into a space of happy expansion.

It's your life, you choose

You can create it entirely to please you. Delete any stuff you may have programmed about 'being selfish' and reframe it in the awareness that only by being true to yourself at your highest level of awareness, your genie awareness, can you become the gift to the world that you are here to be.

Use your feelings as your guide. Your inner being knows what feels right for you. How often when something has gone 'badly' have you remembered that before it happened you had felt uncomfortable about doing it, but had let your logical, rational thinking overrule your intuition, your inner guidance?

Life is meant to feel good. When you're on track, it feels good, whatever your conscious mind might try to tell you.

So, what do you want?

I invite you now to look again at your life wheel and the six areas of your life. Take a new sheet of paper and write the answers to these questions:

1. Pick one area and start to consider the question. What do you want to have, do, be, achieve, experience, or create in this area of your life? It may be something as small or as big as you like.

2. Why do you want this? (If you notice an 'away from' convert it to a 'toward'.) What will this do for you? How will your life be better for having, being or doing this?

3. Create an affirmation to help you retrain your brain and achieve what you want. See Chapter Six to remind you of the process.

4. Do this for each area in turn.

> *You are simply starting a process here. Some areas may be easier than others to identify what you want now. Just note what comes to mind today.*

5. *Practise your affirmations frequently and consistently, remembering to visualise and really feel the experience of having what you are wanting to attract here.*

6. *Notice your feedback.*

7. *Celebrate any and all changes as you notice them.*

Who are your heroes?

There is a saying that who your hero is when you are ten is who you become when you are forty. My hero when I was ten was my teacher, Mrs Bott. She really 'got' who I was and was very encouraging and kind. Even though I was nowhere near when I was forty, I have over the years become much more like her. She is a great role model for me as The Happiness Granny.

I also remember being very inspired when I read that Louise Hay was sixty when she founded Hay House Publishing. At an age when many people are 'winding down', she founded a huge enterprise when she couldn't find a publisher interested in her book. It was very important to her to get her book out to the world and so she published it herself. She had no idea that this would lead to the development of a major publishing house which has benefited many millions of people around the world.

As you contemplate changing your life, or as you start to notice changes that are now occurring, I invite you to consider the heroes in your life. Take a few moments now to bring to mind people who have had a very positive influence in your life. Remember who inspired you when you were ten. Think about people whom you most admire and would like to be like. Who inspires you now? Who is a great role model for you?

Consider who your heroes are and how much you really are like them already. They wouldn't be your heroes if you didn't resonate with them, if you weren't in some way already like them. Maybe you just haven't realised yet. Imagine becoming your own hero as you become aware of all the possibilities you are opening up for yourself. Now is the time to allow fuller expression of your heart's desires.

Albert Einstein also said, "Imagination is everything. It is the preview of life's coming attractions."

What are you imagining?

CHAPTER TEN

Letting Your Genie out

I have written this book because I care. I care passionately about you and all my readers having access to tools and information which can make life easier and better, as you allow yourself to become more fully aware and present to all that you can be in this wonderful world, here and now.

When I first heard Wayne Dyer say, "I am an optimist, because I figure I don't know enough to be a pessimist," I thought that was a great take on life. However much we attempt to stand back and get the bigger picture, we just can't stand back far enough to see it all and know for certain how everything fits together.

Being an optimist feels better and the best you can do is to find or create a philosophy that works well for you. There is no one set of rules/truths/beliefs that works for everyone. If you open your mind and your heart you will be drawn towards and draw towards you whatever has meaning and significance for you. Your level of 'success' can be determined by the happiness and joy in your heart and the peace and well-being in your mind.

Part of the limitation humans create in this world comes from a desire to control others. You can't really control others and you can't even completely consciously control your own life. One thing scientists find terrifying is the fact that the more they understand about the universe and how it operates, the more it becomes apparent how little control any of us has.

Make the best you can of whatever comes your way

If you trust that you are part of a positive world, a world with abundant love and opportunities available for you, if you just practise allowing them, then you really can have, do and be whatever you want. There is more going on than you can understand at present, so make the best you can of whatever comes your way.

I am constantly surprised and amazed by people. Some years ago I used to volunteer at a local centre for homeless people. I wanted to do something useful in my local community and helping to prepare and serve lunch seemed a worthwhile thing to do. Also, I used to be afraid when I encountered homeless people with their cider bottles, noisily occupying the pavement. When I notice a fear, I like to do something about it and so it seemed a good idea to actually interact with people like this, rather than cross the street to avoid them.

I see you

One day, as I was clearing the tables, I saw Stephen huddled in the corner. His usual brown paper bag containing a bottle was on the floor by his feet. He looked his familiar unkempt self, as you might expect from someone sleeping rough. I guess he was in his sixties, but it was difficult to tell. "Hello Stephen. How are you today?" was my breezy greeting. Still slumping in his chair and without looking up, he launched into, "I'm a useless piece of shit. I'm just worthless. I'm a waste of space. I'm just shit," and on he went in this fashion.

As he went through this routine, I looked at him in amazement. He was glowing. There was a bright light around him. "That's not what I see," I replied. He tried harder, "Yes, I am, I'm blah, blah, blah." He tried harder and harder to convince me how useless and worthless he was. "I just can't see that," I replied. On he went and the more he tried to get me to buy his story, the brighter he became. Eventually I started laughing. "Well, I see something different," I said gently and genuinely.

Suddenly he sat up, looked up at me with the most intensely bright blue eyes I have ever seen and said calmly as he gestured around him, "No, none of this is real, is it?" "No," I replied. Then he tapped his temple. "What's real is what's in here, isn't it?" "Yes," I agreed. "And we see the truth in people's eyes, don't we?" "Yes."

There was nothing more to say as we looked deeply into each other's eyes, experiencing who we really are, in deep communion with all that is. After a short while we looked away. He slumped down again and I got on with clearing the tables as usual, inwardly very moved by this unexpected happening and the discovery that Stephen was fully aware of the game he was playing in living the life he was living. I just love it when I allow myself to see beyond the story and the superficial, to experience what is real.

As I look out of my window now, I see a line of about forty sheep walking single file along the well trodden path across the field. I don't know about you, but I've never had much of a sheep mentality. I don't necessarily want to be a follower and walk patiently behind someone else. I enjoy leaving the beaten track and creating my own path, wherever that takes me.

We live in a time of rapid development and change: the universe is continuously expanding and changing; our physical world is changing; society is changing; we now have everyday technology which was considered impossible only a few years ago; and there are more opportunities available to you now than at any time in the history of the world.

Are you making the most you can of this phenomenal gift of life on earth that so many people take for granted? The world is made up of unique individuals. You are the one and only you, here to live your life as only you can. No one else can fully appreciate what this means for you. There are many, many inspirational people who can help you, guide you, inform you and many, many more who can provide the contrast for you in your life!

Only you know who and what you are here to be. Whatever help or guidance you get from others, remember that they can only offer guidance through their own human filters and this may vary in helpfulness to you. Some will be a better fit for you than others.

You can learn to allow your own inner-knowing to be your guidance. Go to the banquet of life, enjoy what is offered and let your genie out. Have fun experimenting, be the success you want to be. As you know, you cannot fail, you can only learn more. Edison learned five thousand ways not to make a light bulb before he created the one which changed the world.

It doesn't matter **what** you do in your life. What matters is **how** you do it, that you do it **wholeheartedly**, with as much **love** and **kindness** as you can allow to flow through you.

It's a waste of time and energy to compare yourself with others or your self-imposed expectations of yourself. Give yourself a break. Stop trying to be the person you think you should be and allow yourself to become the person you would love to be, the thought of which makes your heart sing and allows you to feel your own divinity, your own experience of the power of the universe that you are, the power that flows through you, as you, when you allow it to. It feels soooo good!

Whatever you have been doing up until now, I invite you to jump right into this life that you can create for yourself. Create an excellent life for yourself. Remember the four simple steps to excellence: know what you want; be flexible; use your sensory acuity; and take action, whichever path you take. If you do what you love and love what you do, you're on the right track.

Create your vision

One of the most powerful tools you can use to help you on your chosen path to letting your genie out is a vision board. This is a collection of images, pictures, quotes or affirmations to represent your vision of the life you want to create. You can have a lot of fun making one of these for yourself. You then put it in a prominent place where you will see it often and use it to keep reminding you of the life you are imagining and creating. A simple cork board is easy to use – you can just pin on whatever inspires you and you can easily change it or add to it if you wish. Or you may choose to create a fixed collage – a beautiful arrangement of inspiring words and pictures. Or you can buy a program online to create a vision board on your computer.

The point is to enjoy creating it as you let your imagination run free, looking through magazines, brochures, photos, the internet – anywhere you can find inspiration. As you arrange them on your board, really use all your senses to 'experience' how your life is as it includes this. Use all your senses to get the fullest possible experience, really feel it at all levels. Amp it up. Turn up the brightness, turn up the sounds, turn on the feelings. Make it the best it can be, enjoy all these feelings and then let it all go....

Enjoy noticing your vision board whenever you can. If you ever notice yourself feeling less than positive any time you look at it, if your critical mind is taking score and moving into 'why haven't I got it yet?' territory, then change your focus from a feeling of lack to one of delicious anticipation. Get your critical mind out of the way so that you can allow the desired images and feelings to manifest.

Like Anna's 'winner' card, your board will be a constant reminder to your unconscious mind. You can also focus your conscious mind on the resources and strategies you have encountered in this book:

- ♥ *Measure your success by your level of happiness*
- ♥ *Remember that you create your perceptions, thoughts and beliefs*
- ♥ *You can retrain your brain to support your vision*
- ♥ *Honour and appreciate your uniqueness*
- ♥ *Be aware of your life balance*

♥ *Keep life simple*

♥ *Take more responsibility for your life*

♥ *Use your feelings to guide you*

♥ *Notice what state you are in*

♥ *Focus on what you want*

♥ *You have your own inner genie to guide you*

These are all offered for you to choose from and you can pick and mix as you like. Remember what you have enjoyed reading in this book and do more of it. Act on any inspirations and inner promptings from your genie.

During my NLP practitioner training, we were asked to undertake a project of our own choosing to demonstrate our use of what we were learning. I was very in awe of the 'corporate people' in the group who were coming up with plans to revolutionise the organisations in which they worked. I gave myself a hard time for only coming up with the idea of learning to swim. It seemed very insignificant compared with the impressive projects others were planning.

I eventually silenced the internal wrangling when I paid attention and realised just how much of a big deal being unable to swim was for me. I felt very inadequate next to people who loved swimming and we had even had a swimming pool in the garden when our children were young and I hadn't been able to address this. Now it was time for me to do something very meaningful and helpful for myself.

So the ever-helpful Terence accompanied me to the learners' pool on a Sunday morning with all the small children. I applied the NLP I was learning to really notice what I was feeling and doing as I attempted to swim, then took some lessons and was very proud the day I swam one whole length of the pool. For me it was the most meaningful project I could have undertaken at the time.

As you consider your life vision, what is most important is that it fits for you. Comparing yourself with others is pointless. There isn't another you. Your inner knowing, your genie, will be guiding you, if you allow it to. You may choose to play small in terms of a humble role in life, but your light will shine out for others to see if you allow it to, whatever your lifestyle, occupation, status, income or perceived place or importance in the world.

You may choose a large stage to play on and directly influence or inspire many, many people. You may decide to create a legacy to leave to the world, that your life will be remembered. In the bigger scheme of things, none of these is more important than others. What is important is that you are doing what you love and loving what you are doing, and that in what you are doing you are allowing the flow of creative energy in line with who you are.

All roads lead to Rome

Marianne Williamson also said, "You are here to make manifest the glory of God." For a long time I just didn't 'get' the expression 'glory of God'. It just didn't mean anything to me. I have my own version of God as it seems to me, without the limiting and often less than helpful dogma that go with religions. For me, it's simply a word for the unfathomable intelligence, the creative power of the universe, the source of all, pure loving energy, whatever you want to call that unifying and all-pervasive energy which creates worlds and everything in them.

It amuses me when people talk of God creating man in his image. I prefer the idea that, in the attempt to articulate and describe this concept, man created

God in *his* image, hence some of the less appealing attributes accorded to a 'religious' God.

I had wanted to visit Rome for many years and one Christmas our son gave us the gift of a trip to Rome. When we arrived, I was overwhelmed by the beauty of the buildings with so much gilt and marble and opulence, by the magnificent works of art everywhere we went, by the enormity of Rome and what is there.

One day we walked into yet another fabulously decorated church and a service was taking place in a small chapel to one side. As I think about it now, I am reliving the experience. As I am approaching the chapel in this wonderfully ornate place, I hear a choir of beautiful voices soaring up to the exquisitely painted ceiling. I am in total sensory overload. This is absolutely blissful and far more than I can comprehend. A sudden realisation strikes me - **this** is what the glory of God means to me. The craftsmen involved in the building allowed the creative energy to flow through their hands, their skills, and inspire them to co-create this magnificent building. The skills of the craftsmen inspired and guided by the source of all, by their genies.

Now the singers are joining this creation and I, too, in my appreciation am completely in the flow of this energy. It is a blissful state of connection and knowing. A wonderfully uplifting experience and also very grounded, enjoying the best of both worlds, the physical and the non-physical.

You are here to have the best of both worlds

If you wish, you can experience and be aware of the interconnection of all, the great mystery beyond our comprehension, but always available for us to experience; and you can be grounded in this physical world of being human, with all the delights and fun that brings.

Whether you believe that you have chosen this life before you come here or whether you believe something completely different doesn't matter. Either way, you have choices. They may not always, or ever, be the choices you like, but you always have some choice in this world. You always have available to you the choice of consciously choosing your thoughts, knowing that they become beliefs which create your reality.

You can choose to step up and play a part you wish to play in the world, in the wider community, if that's important to you. You can choose to simply enjoy all that life has to offer. You can shine your light and, as Mahatma Gandhi suggested, be the change you wish to see in the world, if that inspires you.

Whatever your reality, I wish you a life of ever-increasing happiness, joy and prosperity in the choices you are making, the story you are living and the awareness that you are much, much more than you think.

Bless Your Heart

ABOUT THE AUTHOR

Shirley Crichton is a gifted and well-respected coach and mentor, a specialist in helping people to live happier, more positive and successful lives, whatever their circumstances.

For over twenty years she has developed her own model, which is now a synthesis of positive thinking, NLP, psychology, metaphysics, energy work and spiritual teachings, with healthy doses of common sense and humour thrown in.

Shirley is passionate about encouraging and inspiring clients from all walks of life to see beyond their own story, their own perceived limitations, to expand their awareness and get the bigger picture of who they really are and can be in this life. She has helped and influenced many thousands of people and loves witnessing them letting their genies out and discovering that they really can start living the life of their dreams.

Living in a beautiful Northamptonshire village, Shirley works with clients face-to-face, by telephone or by Skype, interspersed with walking, gardening, learning from her grandchildren and exploring the wider world, wherever her curiosity takes her.

Some More Resources I Recommend

Books

Esther & Jerry Hicks	*Ask And It Is Given*
Jill Bolte Taylor	*My Stroke Of Insight*
Joe Vitale	*Zero Limits*
Lola Jones	*Things Are Going Great In My Absence*
Louise Hay	*You Can Heal Your Life*
Miranda Macpherson	*Boundless Love*
Napoleon Hill	*Think And Grow Rich*
Sue Stone	*Love Life, Live Life*

Newspaper

Positive News	*Subscribe at www.positivenews.org.uk*

Website

Shirley's Website	*www.TheHappinessGranny.com*

Can I Help You?

I would be delighted to hear from you if you think I may be able to help you in any way.

You can find out more about my work as a coach and mentor at

www.TheHappinessGranny.com

Do, please, let me know your thoughts on this book, share any stories you have or ask any questions you'd like me to answer.

email **Shirley@TheHappinessGranny.com**